SHAME!
and Masculinity

T0284931

PLURAL
Valiz, Amsterdam

SHAME!
and Masculinity
Ernst van Alphen (ed.)

With contributions by:

Ernst van Alphen
Lorenzo Benadusi
Jeannette Christensen
Marlene Dumas
Adeola Enigbokan
Tijs Goldschmidt
Arnoud Holleman
Hans Hovy
Natasja Kensmil
Wahbie Long
Nalini Malani
Maaike Meijer
Philip Miller
Andrea Pető
Lotte Lara Schröder
Artur Żmijewski
Ina van Zyl

CONTENTS

SHAME! and Masculinity

Jeannette Christensen, *La reproduction interdite*, 2013

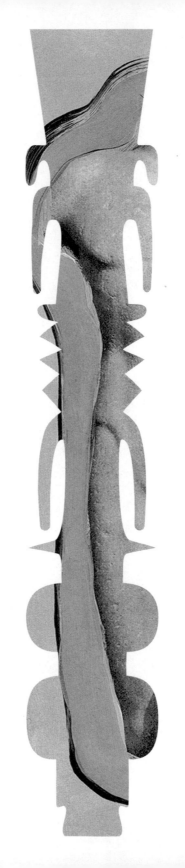

WHEN SHAME AND MASCULINITY COLLUDE AND COLLIDE
Introduction

Ernst van Alphen

1. www.theguardian.com/ film/2014/jan/04/steve-mcqueen-my-painful-childhood-shame?CMP= share_btn_link.

After having made the film *12 Years a Slave*, Steve McQueen was interviewed by Decca Aitkenhead for *The Guardian*. The title of the interview was 'Steve McQueen: My hidden shame'. The painful secret behind his shame is the history of slavery. When the interviewer asks him if he feels angry about this history of black people, he is puzzled and baffled by this question and answers: 'Angry? No. You feel hurt that someone did such things, but angry? No. Painful, sure. Hurt, absolutely. I do not know if that can be seen as anger. Not to say that I am not angry with injustice, of course—and slavery is a huge injustice. But thinking about it that way? No.'[1] McQueen makes a distinction between slavery as injustice and slavery as a painful past experience that still hurts him personally. This painfulness makes him shameful.

Although slavery officially, that is politically and juridically, belongs to the past, it remains part of our societies. Wahbie Long's contribution to this volume explains well in what sense slavery continues to hurt people and to make them shameful. He explains the importance of a universal quality that the ancient Greeks called *thymos*: 'the part of the soul that craves recognition of dignity'. He writes:

Human beings, that is, seek recognition from their peers, and when they do not receive it, one of two things happens. If they feel undervalued, they become resentful, and if they reckon within themselves a failure to meet the standards of others, they feel ashamed. Human beings are not satisfied with only food and shelter; they also want *respect*.[2]

2. Wahbie Long, 'Shame, Envy, Impasse and Hope: The Psychopolitics of Violence in South Africa', this volume, p. 153–177.

The reason why Steve McQueen feels shameful and hurt by slave history can thus be explained by the fact that this past implies the denial of respect to black people. And since racism is still a structural element of our societies, many black people also keep feeling shameful about how they fail to meet the white standards of our society. Slavery was an extreme phenomenon which, however, continues to exist as a structural, systemic invalidating of marginalized groups.

In recent years we have seen two societal outcries that can be explained by shame and the denial of respect to certain people or groups. First of all, the Me Too movement, initiated by women, joined by men, who finally refused to be silent about being made shameful by sexual violence and abuse. Second, the very recent anti-racism protests after George Floyd, a black man, died when a white policeman kneeled on his neck for nearly nine minutes. Although this violent death happened in the American city of Minneapolis (Minnesota), the protests were worldwide and continued for several weeks. The so-called Black Lives Matter movement already existed long before George Floyd was killed, but was fuelled by new energy. The name of this movement is first of all a response to the systematic violence of the American police against black people. This violence is performed by killing them. But Black Lives Matter can also be read as a request for respect: they are asking for respect and dignity that has so far been denied to them. This is, in fact, the precondition for not being killed anymore.

When Black Lives Matter is read as a request for respect and dignity, it becomes understandable that the anti-racism protests were worldwide. These protests are not just acts of solidarity with the black victims of police violence in the United States. After all, the police practices in most European countries and in Australia are not as

ABUSE

3. Myrna Goldenberg, 'Different Horrors, Same Hell: Women Remembering the Holocaust', in *Thinking the Unthinkable: Meanings of the Holocaust*, ed. Roger S. Gottlieb (Mahwah, NJ: Paulist Press, 1990), pp. 150–166.

extremely violently racist as they are in the United States. This difference suggests that anger expressed by these protests all over the world is motivated by solidarity with a societal injustice that characterizes the United States. But it is a relative difference. Although this extreme structural racist violence is perhaps first of all characteristic of the country of which Donald Trump is the 45th and current president, the denial of respect and dignity to black people is a worldwide structural phenomenon. The anger was not just motivated by solidarity with others in another country, although that was certainly also the case, but also by the feeling of being shameful because of the continuous denial of respect, personally and collectively.

Although the Greek concept of *thymos* seen as the 'the part of the soul that craves recognition of dignity' is seen as a universal need and craving, it does not mean that men and women experience this need in the same way and with the same intensity. This is why this volume explores the different ways in which shame colludes and collides with one specific gender, namely masculinity. I will explain this difference in the role of dignity in the construction of femininity and masculinity by using the example of another case of systemic, deadly violence, the Holocaust.

Survival in the concentration camps did not only depend on luck and on how deadly the conditions in the respective camps were, but also on how resistant subjects were. Although subjectivity as such was broken consistently in all respects, one can wonder if this corroding of subjectivity was equally annihilating for everyone. Myrna Goldenberg's argument in her article 'Different Horrors, Same Hell: Women Remembering the Holocaust', that the camp situation was less immediately deadly for many women than for most of the men, can be understood from this perspective.[3] In Western patriarchal society (but also in many others) masculine subjectivity depends much more extremely on the construction of an independent, initiating subject. When subjectivity has to be abjured, and that was the case in order to survive, masculinity is impaired in its essence.

This gender difference in constructions of subjectivity can even explain the fact that in the camps men died much sooner than women. Goldenberg points out that life in the camps was usually much harder for women than for men. Adult men were treated relatively better, because they could be better used as labourers. Yet in 1943, for example, three times as many men than women died in Ravensbrück. Goldenberg suggests that this can be explained by the fact that men were less able than women in 'killing the self in order to survive'. Women could more easily renounce their subjectivities, because in the often orthodox cultures they came from the independence and strength of their subjectivity had been limited anyway.

> ... and being less dependent on inflated egos, as men were, when these egos cracked and were swept away, women recovered faster and with less bitterness.[4]

This view confirms the idea that the construction of masculinity differs from that of femininity and that the role of respect and dignity is more crucial for survival for men than for women. Of course, the Holocaust ended 75 years ago, and a lot has been done since then to make men and women socially more equal. Still, I contend that the construction of masculinity is more vulnerable to the denial of respect and dignity than that of femininity, and that the collusions and collisions between shame and masculinity are more intimate and intense than those between shame and femininity.[5]

Conventionally, the dignity of men depends on two issues: their sexuality and their authority, in other words: their power. And usually those two are closely related to or embedded in each other. Their sexuality is then literally 'overpowering', and in the words of Leo Bersani, their authority depends on a 'phallisizing of the ego'.[6] In this volume male sexuality and male authority are both addressed in their intimate relation to shame. Some of the contributions, such as my own, will mainly focus on sexuality while others address authority, such as the one by Maaike Meijer. The contribution of Wahbie Long on the role of shame and envy in South Africa, is at first sight not dealing with masculinity at all. However, because of my contention that the collusions and collisions between shame and masculinity are more prevalent and intense than between shame and femininity, his essay is implicitly primarily about South African masculinities. Lorenzo Benadusi's essay 'Masculinity' is, in contrast, at

4. Joan Ringelheim, quoted in Goldenberg, 'Different Horrors, Same Hell', p. 153.

5. See my book *Caught By History: Holocaust Effects in Contemporary Art, Literature, and Theory* (Stanford, CA: Stanford University Press, 1997).

6. Leo Bersani, 'Is the Rectum a Grave?', in *Aids: Cultural Analysis, Cultural Activism*, ed. Douglas Crimp (Cambridge, MA: MIT Press, 1988), pp. 197-222.

7. See Eve Kosofsky Sedgwick, *Touching Feeling: Affect, Pedagogy, Performativity* (Durham, NC: Duke University Press, 2003); Tim Dean, *Unlimited Intimacy: Reflections on the Sub-Culture of Barebacking* (Chicago, IL: The University of Chicago Press, 2009).

POWER

first sight not dealing with shame, but just with masculinity in fascist Italy at the beginning of the last century. However, discussing the discrepancy between the virile ideals of masculinity in Italian fascism and 'real' men in those days, he lays bare the cause of the production of shame in men in those days.

What makes the Me Too movement and the anti-racism protests so powerful and impressive is that people speak up not just out of solidarity, but also out of their very personal experiences, feelings, and conditions. It is one of the reasons why this book does not only consist of scholarly, argumentative essays, but also of personal testimonies about experiences in which shame and masculinity connect. It is in these testimonies and stories that we see it happen, the collusion or collision. The contributions by Tijs Goldschmidt, Adeola Enigbokan, and Philip Miller address the issue of shame and masculinity in this personal, testimonial mode. A third genre that this book contains are visual essays and one sound piece, by a diversity of artists. These essays should not be seen as visual or audio illustrations of the issues at stake, but as visual or aural thinking, making their argument by means of visual images or sound. Artists who contributed to this book in this way are Jeannette Christensen, Marlene Dumas, Hans Hovy, Natasja Kensmil, Nalini Malani, Philip Miller, Artur Żmijewski, and Ina van Zyl.

But as many have argued, shame is not a static affect, it is a dialectical process that evokes pride, dignity, and even shamelessness.[7] What these dialectical opposites have in common is that both can result in anger. Shaming somebody or a specific group is often related to anger; people use shaming in order to punish people. And as the recent anti-racism protests demonstrate, being made shameful can make people angry. This volume will address both manifestations of shame. The act of inflicting shame on other people, as well as being inflicted by shame and feeling the experience of isolation by shame. Whereas the first part of the book is especially devoted to shaming and the slogan 'Shame on You!', the second part deals with the hyper-self-reflexive experience of isolation in shame.

In my own essay I develop the issues of the different connections between shame and masculinities, in close engagement with the various artworks invoked. The affect of shame itself in its social ramifications, its distinction from guilt, and its impact on the sense of self, of who one is, has had a place in the history of visual representations of human bodies, most clearly in the genre of the nude. But also other manifestations of shame demonstrating the shaming, shamelessness, and shameful-ness that exist in different cultural contexts are addressed. The book as a whole offers a wide opening-up of this affect, so frequently felt and so rarely discussed and analyzed.

I am very grateful to Marlene Dumas for our discussions about the male nude and other hot issues.

Arnoud Holleman, *Family and Friends*, 2002
pencil, serie of seven drawings, 29.7 x 21 cm each

ARTUR ŻMIJEWSKI

Gestures, 2019, chronophotography

SHAME! and Masculinity

Artur Żmijewski   *Gestures*, 2019, chronophotography

SHAME! and Masculinity

Artur Żmijewski   *Gestures*, 2019, chronophotography

Artur Żmijewski   *Gestures*, 2019, chronophotography

UP AND UP, DOWN AND OUT

Tijs Goldschmidt

Place 1 / Throwing Stones

I was about eleven years old. I was one of the first girls to sprout breasts. Proudly I showed the tufts of hair in my armpits, as proof that in that more secret spot there was also hair, more hair, to be found. I was smart, cheerful, advanced for my age, and my friends appreciated me. I came up with exciting things to do, like wandering to the raised sand plain behind the school, where I had discovered a barn that was no longer used. There had been a bunch of small allotment gardens there once.

In that decrepit barn we knew we would not be spied upon by all those we believed to always keep an eye on us; with good reason, of course. What we thought and did was of the utmost importance. I told stories I had invented and which I expanded on the spot, and not only that; when back home I wrote them down in a green school notebook with lines on the pages. Stories about other girls who were no longer welcome in our club. Enumerations of their lapses. Without knowing it, I was plagiarizing Christ: I predicted who among us would soon betray me.

We held our meetings preferably in the barn, but during lunch breaks there was not enough time, so we just hung out in the schoolyard. Half-hidden behind a thick chestnut tree, close to the igloo-shaped climbing frame, we gossiped about those who weren't there, we giggled, or I read my stories. When the girls were distracted by boys playing soccer I refused to go on reading.

Our password was 'snow peas'. No one remembered why and when the password had been taken up, but everyone pretended it was totally clear and had to be like that. Whoever raised their little finger, ever so slightly, almost imperceptibly, and said 'snow peas' at the same time, belonged in the group and had nothing to worry about for the time being. When *I* said 'snow peas', my friends knew that I had brought something. I regularly stole money from my mother's purse to buy key-shaped liquorice, 'black-on-white' finger dip and other sweets, which I handed out. My status rose rapidly. Up and up.

One glorious day, paviours came for a 'refurbishing', as had been announced in school, of pavement and schoolyard. The lead-grey cobblestones were pried lose one by one, to be replaced by neat grey paving stones. The boys had moved to a small lawn nearby to play their soccer games, because during the refurbishing no soccer playing was allowed, but we just kept hanging out in the schoolyard. One morning, coming out of school in high spirits, the paviours had gone for their lunch break. They had stretched a large tarpaulin over the climbing frame and tied it at the corners, with a gorgeous tent as a result. In it, they had left their sledgehammers, shovels, ropes, leather gloves, and knee pads. 'Do not touch, please!' had been written in large letters on a piece of cardboard. For a while we played in and around our igloo. As soon as thaw would set in we'd be compelled to trek further in our search for spoon leaf. Preventing scurvy was our primary concern. At some point two girls had stayed behind in the igloo, one of whom was my best friend. I picked up one of the loose cobblestones that lay everywhere, and threw it against the tarpaulin. From the igloo came laughter. Up and up. I felt encouraged to continue, selecting heavier and heavier stones, throwing them harder and harder against the canvas. Each time this resulted in exuberant laughter from the tent. Until suddenly they fell silent and my friend appeared. She held her hands against her forehead, looked repeatedly at her fingers that had turned red, and she was bleeding heavily. When, back in the bright sunlight again, she saw the blood streaming over her hands, she burst into sobs. Panicking, supported by some friends, she went inside. I was not allowed to help, they snapped at me. They pushed me away, down and out. I cursed myself, I had been too wild again.

The caretaker cleaned the wound and put iodine

on it. 'Not too bad', he said encouragingly, but our teacher, who had joined the group, burst out furiously: 'How often have I warned you? After the break, you will go to all the classrooms with her to show what you have done.' She twisted my cheek between thumb and index finger and continued: 'So, this is how you treat your best friend.' I had a vague feeling that this was unfair. We went from classroom to classroom. With each enforced confession my face turned redder and more subdued – it was torture. All this time, my friend said nothing to me, and every time I tried to hold her arm, she pulled it away forcefully. 'Don't touch me.'

She persevered in this for weeks, while the other girls avoided and ignored me. Down and out. I held back and behaved decently and controlled. Shame shaves us for group life.

Place 2 / Remembering my Begetter

He also tried it with my brothers.

No, I never told you.

He also tried it with my brothers, my older brother, but also with my younger one. All in the same time period.

I prefer not to talk about this. It distresses me again immediately. I thought it was over, after many years, but this is how I know it: that is typically shame. It does not follow you around but it is lurking in your own head. It came in there without being invited, and patiently waits for its opportunity. And then suddenly it strikes, flares up and paralyzes. Shame makes one small-minded and conformist. Before you know it, you cry with the wolves, no, with the lap dogs and cowardly barking ones. Shame shaves us for group life. Please, let's stop talking about it.

*Okay. That's true. He also tried it with my two brothers, but they didn't let him. My younger brother neither. They never relinquished control. They said, stop, no further. Up and up. No, then take me. I didn't dare. Yes, there were reasons for that. It's easy for you to say there were none, but this is how I experienced it. I wanted to disappear, to eclipse, to never return. Down and out.

He also tried it with my two brothers. Even with my younger brother, but he didn't let him. I did. It happened in the bathroom, always in the bathroom. Are you sure you want to hear this? I prefer not to talk about it.

I still see myself standing there, about thirteen years old. Naked, in the shower. My father entered the bathroom, undressed, and joined me. He soaped me. Kneaded my shoulders, drew long loops of foaming soap on my breast, belly, along my back, to the upper edge of my buttocks. Going down and down with his soap drawings, as if he was tying me up. Not really unpleasant. Meanwhile he came closer and closer. I saw his sex grow stiff. I took a step back. He dropped the soap and groped my dick, while teaching that I should keep it very clean. Then he demonstrated how to do that with his own, and became harder still.

Nothing, I did nothing, I froze, was speechless. I meant to speak to him, tell him I didn't want this. I opened and closed my mouth, a wrasse gasping for air, but what I wanted to say didn't come out. I could not. Where were my brothers? Where was my mother? Down and out.

I surrendered, let him do with me what he wanted, hoping that it would be over more quickly that way. 'Our secret', he called it, and ended with the words: 'I trust you'.

It went on for six months, several times a week. I did not dare speak about it to anyone, I kept my mouth shut. As soon as my mother went into town and my brothers left the house to go and play tennis, I knew the moment had come again. Sometimes I didn't manage to get out fast enough. I still hate tennis, it disgusts me. I can't bear to see or hear a tennis ball. Hearing one smack of a racket against a ball brings it back. No, he never apologized, not even on his death bed. One day he had bitten me there, until bleeding. That was the last time. Let's stop talking about it.

I withdraw within myself. I avoid everyone. Less and less they see me, address me, greet me. I barely greet others myself, so that is not so strange. I have become a persona non grata in my own head. I don't let myself in anymore. No longer welcome. I don't want anything to do with me.

SHAME! and Masculinity

Down and out. I understand the others very well. Let's stop talking about it.

For a week I walked around with a bitten ... . It started festering. I hesitated too long to go to the GP, a friend of my father if you believe it. I was terrified to be unmasked. When I ended up going after all, he said: 'Where did you get that? You are not in a seminary, are you?' 'My father, my father', but I said nothing, out of fear and shame. I thought of our 'secret' and of that he had said 'I trust you'. Paradoxical as it may sound, I was proud of that. I didn't want to betray his trust and by keeping silent I protected him. He had not done it on purpose. Scared by a sound on the stairs he had feared my mother would enter the bathroom. His canine hit my ... Aiii. Days afterwards I was sitting in school with a throbbing sex. I felt my heartbeat there. A rhythmic reminiscence of the most painful incident of a long series, while the teacher of classics explained what the conjunctive meant: 'If only I had been more unyielding.' Although my father is long dead, he is on my mind every day. He used me to practice for his coming-out; the only one of his sons who did not resist.

Place 3 / Red Fingers

It is a stylish hall with an eighteenth-century ceiling full of garlands with bunches of grapes, and playing putti looking down on us from above. The luxurious villa serves as the temporary location of the conservatory, until the new building at the edge of Lille is finished.

One of the members of the admission committee invites me to take place behind the grand piano and to start. It is the first time I am allowed to play on a grand piano, something I have been looking forward for years. But I cannot enjoy it, since the unmasking is upcoming. I will mess up, no doubt about it. In order to have a chance to be one of the few to be admitted, I must play three pieces, just like the dozens of other candidates. I am one of the last ones, on that sweltering day. I had been sitting for hours in a waiting room with the windows closed until my turn would come.

The committee members, two women and three

men, middle-aged, are sitting at a long wooden table at some distance from the piano. I sit straight, take two deep breaths, and begin to play. Immediately it occurs to me that of course, I should have nodded at them first, before I began. Stupid.

I am just into it when one of the committee members stands up. He pushes his chair backwards on the parquet floor, which creaks. I continue to play, but find it very hard to keep concentrating, and I look sideways. He walks carefully, strangely bent over, towards the piano, each time raising one knee higher than necessary before landing his toes on the parquet. He demonstrates excessively that he doesn't want to disturb me, like someone who has arrived late in a concert hall. I continue playing, look sideways again, and notice that he is making grimaces directed at the other committee members. Is he mocking me?

Almost immediately, a second committee member follows, grinning, imitating his awkward walk, while she holds her stretched index finger straight up in front of her closed mouth. She makes the impression that she can burst into laughter at any moment. Swiftly, less cautiously, the other committee members now also get up and walk towards the grand piano. They share something that escapes me, but doubtlessly concerns my pitiful presence or play. I blush. Suddenly I see myself sitting on that piano stool. What an insane idea to want to audition here. How did I become so arrogant? A kid with excessively high ambitions he won't ever be able to make true. He sees what they think of him. Up and up, down and out.

A honking car in the street called me back to order. Stay calm, they had not said anything yet. Up and up. Two committee members were now standing behind me, two to my right and one was leaning with her elbow on the piano and was looking at how my fingers were gliding over the keys. Were the others watching my fingers as intensely as she did? All that collective attention to my fingers. Even the piercing looks of the plastered putti contributed.

I looked at my fingers and saw that they, too, were blushing. Down and out. If only I had never won that music contest, went through my head, then this would never have happened. I thought of Mrs. Dupré who, the first time I came for a lesson again after the youth contest asked me to follow her to her private quarters, where the grand piano was. 'That is quite different from the teaching piano', she had frequently emphasized. Her grand piano that no one was allowed to touch, except her sister, a well-known pianist, 'Listen', she said, while putting on a disc. 'Listen to the way my sister plays this Hayden sonata.' We listened for a few minutes, after which she lifted the arm from the disc and pulled it backwards to stop the device. Click. She looked at me and said: 'Do you hear what I mean?' I said nothing. 'Do you hear the difference with your play?' I nodded, looking at the floor. 'That's already something,' she pursued. 'You have a pounding touch.' Down and out.

I wanted to disappear, just as I do now. My fingers tingled, while I still continued playing. The putti fooling around, the grinning committee members, they all looked at my fingers, which by now had turned bright red. Shame shaves us for group life. I made mistakes, stopped playing, and dropped my hands in my lap, despairing. 'You will never play like my sister', is what Dupré had wanted to say at the time. Living is doing audition. Shame daubs the fingers red. It splatters the red on your cheeks up to far behind your ears and deep inside your neck. Where looks direct themselves, there the red follows irrevocably.

Originally published in Dutch in *De Gids* 173 (2010), pp. 759–765.

Dutch musician/composer Maarten Altena explored feelings of shame together with Tijs Goldschmidt in his piece for tenor and instruments *Up and Up/Down and Out*. The part 'Red Fingers' (based on the text by Tijs Goldschmidt) was performed by the ASKO/Schönberg Ensemble in 2010.

WITHDRAWAL

Tijs Goldschmidt

SHAME AND MASCULINITY IN VISUAL CULTURE

Ernst van Alphen

1. Eve Kosofsky Sedgwick, *Touching Feeling: Affect, Pedagogy, Performativity* (Durham, NC: Duke University Press, 2003), p. 36.

Recent Me Too scandals have led to two powerful affects in people: anger and shame. Those two affects are intimately related, because anger is often expressed by inflicting shame on the person at whom the anger is directed, as in 'Shame on you!' We punish people by making them shameful. Whereas the former affect of anger and 'Shame on you!' is directed against the perpetrators, the affect of shame is much more difficult to locate. It can be experienced by victims, bystanders, as well as by perpetrators, and people who identify with one of these positions. But because of the fact that Me Too perpetrators are most often male, the affect of shame is especially felt by men. In order to broaden this and better understand how masculinities have been shaped by feelings of shame, I will explore the different manifestations of shame, in intimate relation with its repercussions on masculinity.

Cultural analyst Eve Sedgwick has explained the nature, origin, and effect of shame most clearly:

> The shame response, when it appears, represents the failure or absence of the smile of contact, a reaction to the loss of feedback from others, indicating social isolation and signalling the need for relief of that situation.[1]

Because the relationality with the other person is broken or no longer under control, a painful individuation is the outcome. This implies that shame concerns a sense of self.

The symptoms of the fallen face and blushing skin indicate the trouble felt when a circuit of communication is broken and, at the same time, a desire emerges to reconstitute the interpersonal link. Sedgwick's explanation also makes clear how shame differs from guilt, an affect which is sometimes difficult to distinguish from shame. Shame attaches to and sharpens the sense of what one is, whereas guilt attaches to what one *does*.[2]

Being affected by shame means that one is affected by who or what one is, although one may or may not be certain as to what that is exactly. That is why shame is often considered to be the affect that most clearly defines the space in which a sense of self will develop. But as explained before, this sense of self is the result of a failure; it indicates that the effective contact with another person has been broken. Therefore, shame can be thought of as the inability to effectively arouse the other person's positive reactions to one's communications. But this goes in two directions: shame derives from a relation of sociability, and at the same time aims to achieve a restoration of sociability. The painful individuation which shame entails is intimately related to those actions or affects that are its negation:

> Shame effaces itself; shame points and projects; shame turns itself inside out; shame and pride, shame and dignity, shame and self-display, shame and exhibitionism are different interlinings of the same glove.[3]

In other words, shame is the affect located on the threshold between introversion and extroversion. Although shame as such results in introversion, this painful introversion can be worked through and overcome by explicit and overt extrovert behaviour.

In what follows I will explore these different manifestations of shame in the direction of introversion as well as extroversion, by first focusing on the role of shame and shamelessness[4] in the main traditions of Western art. Such an historical exposure is necessary for a better understanding of recent representations of masculinity. I will especially pay attention to the male nude in the Western tradition of art. It will turn out that shame and dignity are

2. Ibid., p. 37.

3. Ibid., p. 38.

4. Although in everyday usage words like 'shameless' and 'shameful' have mainly negative connotations, in this essay they are used in a more 'neutral' sense, as in 'with or without shame attached'.

intimately related, not as binary opposites, but as the one as a condition for the other: without having felt shame the display of dignity is not really possible.

Nakedness seems to be no problem at all in Western art. The nude is an old and established genre. From the classical period we know first of all the male nude. In the course of history, it seems that people became less comfortable with the male nude, but that is largely compensated by the rise of the female nude. The female nude also originates in the Greek classical period, although it emerged several centuries after the male nude had been introduced. So, at first sight nudity does not seem to be a shameful problem; it is not restricted by taboos. However, this is a misconception. How is masculinity represented through the male nude? How is femininity depicted through the female nude? What are the differences? Nudity is in one way or another always connected to two issues, both to do with sexuality. First of all, male sexuality differs from female sexuality and as a result, the male nude is shaped differently than the female nude. Second, sexuality is always embedded in power relations, in difference in power, that is. This difference in power reflects itself in visual traditions not only in how

Cnidus Aphrodite, Roman copy after a Greek original of the 4th century

Praxiteles, *Knidian Aphrodite*, c. 340 BC, Roman copy

Capitole Venus, Roman copy of Hellenistic original, c. 120 BC, Rome

scenes are depicted, but also in the relation between image and viewer. The question is, who is the subject of the look and who is its object, in other words, who is looking at whom? And who is in a shameful position: the subject who is voyeuristically looking, or the object of the voyeuristic look?

I will address these issues by relying on a brilliant essay by the American feminist art historian Nanette Salomon. She published this text in 1996 in the volume *Generations and Geographies in the Visual Arts: Feminist Readings*, edited by another famous feminist art historian, Griselda Pollock.[5] Salomon writes her history of the male and the female nude by first focusing on one of the most persistent traditions in depictions of the female nude, that of the so-called *Venus pudica*. This tradition concerns the idealized representation of a female nude, who covers her pubic area with her hand. This pose or gesture has its origin in sculptures by the Greek sculptor Praxiteles, from the fourth century before Christ. His *Aphrodite* is the paradigmatic work in relation to which the whole *Venus pudica* tradition from the classical period to the present can be understood.

This tradition has become standard, so that this pose or gesture has become completely 'normal' and naturalized. As a result, one does not recognize it anymore as a specific pose or gesture: it seems natural. The question that arises is: how is femininity constructed by means of this gesture, since this gesture is not at all natural?

As I already said, in Western art the female nude has a much later origin than the male nude, a gap of four centuries. The differences between the male nude and female nude are striking. From the archaic period we know the so-called *kouroi*, athletic young men. These idealized figures depict men as young, naked, and heroic. The corresponding *korai*, in contrast, are dressed in elaborate draperies. Salomon formulates the difference between kouroi and korai as follows:

> The male figure is portrayed as coherent and
> rational from within; the female figure is portrayed
> as attractive from without; the male body is dynam-
> ically explored as an internal logic, organic unity,

5. Nanette Salomon, 'The Venus Pudica: Uncovering Art History's "Hidden Agendas" and Pernicious Pedigrees', in *Generations and Geographies in the Visual Arts: Feminist Readings*, ed. Griselda Pollock (London: Routledge, 1996), pp. 69–87.

Kleobis and Biton, c. 610–600 BC

Kroisos Kourois, c. 650–500 BC

Kouroi, between 640–480 BC

6. Ibid., p. 71.

7. See Norman Bryson, 'Géricault and Masculinity', in *Visual Culture: Images and Interpretations*, ed. Norman Bryson, Michel Holly, and Keith Moxey (Hanover, NH: Wesleyan University Press, 1994), pp. 228–259.

the female body is treated as an external surface for decoration.[6]

The fact that an idealized notion of youthful nakedness was exclusively reserved for the male subject has a lot to do with the Greek definition of beauty, where beauty was an exclusively male attribute and had an important role in male homosexual desire, which was privileged. So, men are depicted fully naked, their penises are exhibited without any restrictions, not covered as the *Venus pudica* does with her pubic area.

But what characterizes the Greek and Roman traditions of the male nude is that the penis is slightly reduced in size. This is of course a difficult issue, because of the underlying norm: what is the standard size of a penis? Unstable as penises are, opinions about what the standard size is can differ. But in art history the established idea is that classical penises are reduced in size. In general, that is correct, because in the tradition of the Greek male nude impressively big penises do not exist in idealized depictions of men.[7] Of course, men are sometimes depicted with a grotesquely big penis in classical art also, but those representations are not idealized, but rather comical. In order to represent male beauty convincingly the penis has to be reduced in size. A result of this reduction is that explicit references to male sexuality are absent. The penis is represented in the same casual way as knees, elbows, or noses are. These sculptures seem to say that there is really nothing special about these penises. Insofar as these male nudes suggest sexuality, the men themselves seem to be completely unaware of their sexuality. There is no display of what they 'carry', but also no shame. The lack of awareness of their sexuality can be seen, however, as a displacement of the potential shamefulness of male sexuality. By not being aware of one's sexuality, there is no potential shamefulness either.

Precisely this lack of self-consciousness differs radically from what goes on in the tradition of the *Venus pudica*. The women in these depictions are highly self-conscious of their sexuality. But they are not only self-conscious, they are also vulnerable, because exposed; but exposed to what? This is also suggested by this very simple

Polykleitos, *Discophoros*, c. 460s BC

Ernst van Alphen

gesture of the hand covering the pubic area. Whereas men in all their nakedness are not depicted as sexual beings, women are depicted, not only as utterly sexual, but also as being sharply aware of that fact.

The right hand covering the pubic area tells a very specific story. It constructs a story of anxiety in anticipation of events to which it should offer protection. It suggests that these women do not want to be seen. In fact, being seen is here analogous to being raped. With this pose and gesture Praxiteles has not only sent into the world a very particular construction of femininity, but also a specific kind of viewer. When we look at images in the tradition of the *Venus pudica*, the viewer is constructed as a voyeur. We as viewers are turned into Peeping Toms when we marvel before these pictures and sculptures.

In short, whereas during the classical period a depiction of a female nude was for a long time unthinkable because not interesting, the moment that the female nude is born, it emerges in such a way that several scenarios of erotic pleasure are being projected onto the female body. Precisely by covering the pubic area, Praxitiles focuses all attention on what cannot be seen; by hiding it, it becomes extremely desirable to look at or to possess; to own visually or physically.

One more thing about the naming of this tradition in depicting female nudity is relevant for the present discussion. The word 'pudicia' is etymologically related to 'pudenda', a word that means shame as well as genitalia. This telling coincidence of different meanings goes back to the double meaning of the Greek root *aidos*. In the tradition of the *Venus pudica*, however, *pudica* is no longer associated with shame but with modesty. That is a very different sexual story than the one suggested by the term itself and by the female figure's body language and gesture. The gesture then suggests to express modesty instead of anxiety. But in fact, modesty and shame are closely related.

The Greek examples I have provided so far are not enough to speak of a long tradition. But during the Renaissance a revival of classical culture takes place. The genres of the male nude as well as the female nude are being practiced seriously again. During the Middle Ages, the nude was no longer a specified genre, but reserved for

PUDICA

Jeroen Bosch, *The Garden of Earthy Delights*, c. 1490–1510, left panel of the tryptich

Sandro Botticelli, *Birth of Venus*, 1483

Michelangelo, *David*, c. 1501–1504

Donatello, *David*, c. 1440

the representation of Adam and Eve, in Paradise or being driven out of it. Given what happens in that story, shame is relevant. This means, they are shown as either shameless or shamefully covering their genitalia. It is remarkable that Adam too covers his genitalia, in this tradition. The possibility to represent men naked without any suggestion of their sexuality is no longer credible in the Middle Ages. But in the Renaissance the classical differentiation between male and female nude returns. Men again have reduced penises and woman cover their pubic area self-consciously. The Davids of Donatello and of Michelangelo are great examples of this tradition of the male nude, whereas *The Birth of Venus* by Botticelli exemplifies the Renaissance return of the *Venus pudica*. In the case of Boticelli, it is remarkable that the gesture Venus makes has nothing to do with the narrative of the painting: the birth of Venus. If Venus performs this gesture already during her birth, it can only concern an essentialist notion of femininity: as inherently sexual and as self-conscious of that, although allegedly she has just been born.

An important development in the *Venus pudica* tradition is the moment that Venus is going to be depicted horizontally, as in the *Sleeping Venus* of Giorgione and Titian's *Venus of Urbino*. Laying horizontally, the passivity of these Venuses is emphasized. And the covering of the pubic area does not seem to be a conscious gesture, out of anxiety or protection; it is an almost self-evident, unreflective, perhaps even unconscious gesture. The essentialist construction of femininity as inherently sexual is intensified by these horizontal Venuses.

It is this essentializing of femininity as sexual that becomes the target of later critique. One of the first deconstructions of the *Venus pudica* is Edouard Manet's *Olympia*. In Titian's *Venus of Urbino* we still recognize a characteristic that many *Venus pudicas* are acquiring: the rather anxious look of the Classical tradition transforms into a more hypocritical, encouraging look in the direction of the voyeuristic viewer. Although the genitalia are covered, the look tells a different story. Manet's Olympia's look is radically different. When Manet's painting was presented in 1863 in the Parisian Salon, it produced an enormous scandal. Olympia's look was neither anxious, nor encouraging, nor modest. Her look confronts the viewer in an almost brutal way. The hasty, self-evident conclusion is that she has to be a prostitute. But being a prostitute, she cannot be a model for idealized femininity, so the painting should have been refused for the Salon. Her look directs back the voyeuristic gaze of the viewer. He gets a blush of shame on his cheeks, I imagine, because he becomes aware of the fact that he is doing something not very decent. Like the *Venus pudica*, Olympia covers her pubic area, but that is no longer the centre of attention. Her confrontational look has taken central stage. A viewer exposed to such a look can only withdraw or become angry, as did the visitors of the salon in 1863.[8]

Another, later deconstruction of the *Venus pudica* tradition is the following image that can be found on the Web. In this case the male's genitalia are the ones that are covered, instead of the female's. But it is the woman who covers the man's genitalia. The man is still not aware of his own sexuality; the woman is, more than ever. Although there is no reason anymore to cover her own pubic area, there is more reason than ever to cover his. This image can be seen as announcing the Me Too Period in Visual Culture.

On the basis of this very short history of the male and the female nude in Western art one can draw the following conclusions about masculinity. Whereas women are depicted as defined by their sexuality, as sexual beings, in the representation of men their sexuality plays a minor

8. See for an alternative reading of Manet's *Olympia*: Mieke Bal, 'His Master's Eye', in *Double Exposures: The Subject of Cultural Analysis* (London: Routledge, 1996), pp. 255–288.

Giorgione, *Sleeping Venus*, 1510

Titian, *Venus of Urbino*, 1538

Venus Pudica revisited

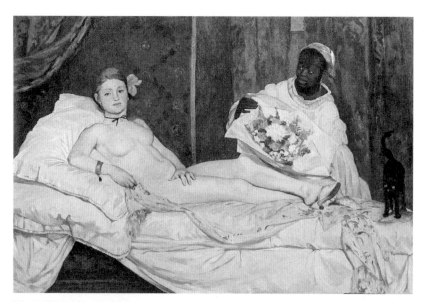

Edouard Manet, *Olympia*, 1863

role. Their genitals do not occupy a special place in the representation of their masculinity; they are comparable with any other body part. And even more importantly: women are always highly self-conscious of their sexuality, whereas men are depicted in such a way that they do not show any awareness of their sexuality. Theirs exists only in the eye of the beholder. This has repercussions for the affect of shame. In visual culture the shameful sexuality of men can be dealt with in two ways. First, by denying shame and showing no signs of any awareness of their sexuality; second, by refusing any representations of shameful male sexuality in the visual domain. This is no option for women; their sexuality is always present in visual culture, as something shameful that should be hidden, following the *Venus pudica* tradition; or as something that should be exploited and exposed shamelessly as an object of desire and more recently also as a subject of desire.

But of course, since the 1960s the second feminist wave has changed a lot in the representation of masculinity in visual culture. Although it has taken some time before the heated, iconoclast discussions of those days about male and female representations resulted in transformations in visual culture, it is now, anno 2020, common to see men in caring roles in advertisements or in films. But although the image of masculinity is no longer the binary opposite of femininity, it is not so clear whether the *role* of male sexuality within masculinity has fundamentally changed. The Me Too scandals of recent years can be seen as a radicalized revival of earlier feminist discussions, a revival with great iconoclast repercussions for the image of masculinity, especially of male sexuality. For this text, I have selected works by a variety of artists, both male and female, in order to explore the issues that for centuries have determined representations of masculinity, especially, but not exclusively, of male sexuality. How self-conscious are men in the depictions of their sexuality? Is their sexuality addressed in a shameful or a shameless way? Is masculinity exclusively assigned to men, or also to women?

The emblem, or opening image of this critical itinerary through art is the work *La Reproduction interdite* by Norwegian artist Jeannette Christensen. The work shows the notorious Norwegian mass killer Anders Behring Breivik from the back, in front of a mirror. The image is

SELF-CONSCIOUSNESS

modelled after the 1937 painting with the same title by the Belgian surrealist artist Magritte, now in the Museum Boijmans Van Beuningen in Rotterdam. Breivik, who killed 77 people in Oslo in 2011 is, indeed, a person 'not to be reproduced'. The book on the mantelpiece has that warning as its title. The image in the mirror is not the mirror image of Breivik in front of the mirror: it is his repetition, as if the mirror refuses to mirror him. The title suggests that real mirror images are not just repetitions. They show or reveal something that the person in front of the mirror can only see in front of the mirror, namely he, as the subject of the look, but now objectified, looking at himself as object. Mirror images are in the most literal sense self-reflective; the subject in front of the mirror looks at himself as an object. That is not the case in Magritte's painting nor in Christensen's image of Breivik. Magritte's painting and Christensen's photograph are not self-reflective; instead they show the inability of self-reflection by repeating the figure in front of the painting. This inability could be the result of shame: Breivik is not able, nor allowed by the artist, to face himself. In the case of the itinerary through art of which it is a part, the failed self-reflection in Christensen's image of Breivik is also a statement about the failure to self-reflect on masculinity and male sexuality. That inability is, however, re-directed by the fact that this image is the opening image of my discussion, and by that positioning, is given special power: it signifies that this reflection reflects on the failure to reflect.

Jeannette Christensen, *Forbidden to Reproduce*, 2018, photograph

Shame on you!

Natasja Kensmil's drawings seem to confront the viewer with a multiplicity of images tumbling across and through each other. The composition of the drawings is not orderly, nor centred. There is no hierarchy between foreground and background. A lack of perspectival regularity means that the viewer's gaze finds no refuge. The view is not guided, leaving the viewer restlessly scanning the surface of the drawing. The bubbling unrest which typifies the work's content is reflected in the act of drawing. All these formal

Natasja Kensmil, *(6)ex, (6)ex, (6)ex*, 2001, drawing, charcoal on paper, 93 x 150 cm

Natasja Kensmil, *Carrousel*, 2001, drawing, charcoal on paper, 93 x 150 cm

9. For more on this artist see my essay 'Drawing Time', in *Natasja Kensmil: Universal Souvenir* (Hengelo: Broekhuis, 2003).

qualities together express a feeling of arousal, incitement and rage: they agitate the anger behind the slogan 'Shame on you!'

The overpowering mass of heterogeneous impressions seems to emerge from the image culture associated with postmodernity. The images emanate from a broad range of current media: from newspapers, magazines, films, and the internet, and particularly from genres which address mass culture such as advertising, pornography, action and crime films. The impressions are already interwoven in the images, which in turn assail the subject.[9]

This might suggest that her drawings all point unequivocally to the actuality of the late twentieth and early twenty-first centuries, which is not the case at all. Kensmil pierces right through the current culture by accentuating the mythical dimension of current mass culture. In this respect, the drawings are ultimately very ambiguous: they both reverberate with actuality, and yet they are timeless in a mythical or archetypical sense. The stratification of the drawings, the fact that new images steadily appear to be applied over earlier ones, that new images constantly appear to be imminent, produces an image of drawing as the production of palimpsests, in an extremely rapid way of proceeding. In Kensmil's case, this characteristic of drawing becomes even more convincing when we consider the huge contrast between her drawings and her paintings. The paintings are also stratified. They consist of physically strong layers of very thickly applied paint. The emphatic materiality of the paint, its viscosity, actually engenders a feeling of *inertia*. An extremely prolonged process coagulates here in the bulk of paint. But on closer inspection the contrast between the drawings and the paintings also takes shape *within* the paintings. The depictions are often graphic; they are applied in light lines over the predominantly dark paint. Here the hand of the painter exercises a technique that is at odds with the inertia of paint. While an image is built up from layers of paint, from bottom to top, the act of drawing is predicated on an opposing technique: it marks a trace which is left behind on a surface. Somethings is applied to whatever already existed by the artist's hand from within the here-and-now.

It is precisely this tension between the rapid

Natasja Kensmil, *Carry Me*, 2001, drawing, charcoal on paper, 102 x 150 cm

Natasja Kensmil, *Lynndie England III*, 2005, drawing, charcoal on paper, 150 x 150 cm

Ernst van Alphen

drawing and the slow painting, both in painting as such and between the two media in which Kensmil works, which ensures that images of actuality bisect so convincingly with a mythical dimension. Kensmil's images are overwhelming, but not just in their visual effect on the viewer. The images' subject matter matches this convergence. It is consistent with situations of violence, temptation, and sexuality. As I mentioned earlier, we recognize images from genres that provide the dominant tones in contemporary popular culture: porn films, crime films and television reporting on war and crime. What these genres have in common is that temptation is suggested as violent and violence as tempting. Increasingly these themes, which appear to be so contrary at first glance, are becoming one diffused territory. Yet this interweaving of violence and temptation is certainly not specific to contemporary popular culture. On the contrary: it is by means of these themes, among others, that Kensmil's work achieves its mythical dimensions.

In ancient stories such as those of Samson and Delilah, Salomé and John the Baptist, Judith and Holofernes (to name just a few from the biblical tradition) the themes of temptation and violence are also intricately intertwined. In the mythical stories Kensmil evokes in her drawings, men and women are well matched. There is never a clichéd scenario with physically strong men and weak women who need to resort to secretive seduction techniques because they are not equipped for violence. In contrast with the biblical stories just mentioned, in Kensmil's drawings one is invariably concerned with groups, even armies of men. And in most cases the women also multiply in the images. The women impress through their strength, and this is precisely what makes them seductive. This is not new with regard to manhood's domineering makeup; in Western notions of femininity it is actually unheard of, however. Because of the difference between powerful men and powerful women, it is clear that the anger behind 'Shame on you' is in these images bestowed by the female figures upon the male figures. Kensmil depicts the collision of a world of men with a world of women. This collision is not being moderated or channelled by stereotyped plans, however, because shamefulness qualifies the male figures. The female figures, in contrast, are just impressive.

10. See also my earlier reading of Marlene Dumas' work: 'Facing Defacement', in *Art in Mind: How Contemporary Images Shape Thought* (Chicago, IL: University of Chicago Press, 2005), pp. 140–161.

Marlene Dumas, *Identity Crisis—Man Confusing Art and Life*, 1993, ink on paper, 32 x 24 cm

Marlene Dumas, *Beauty as Burden*, watercolour, c. 1996, ink, ink wash and acrylic on paper, 50 x 40 cm

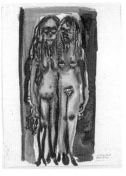

Marlene Dumas, *Two Bearded Beauties*, c. 1996, ink, ink wash and acrylic on paper, 50 x 40 cm

Marlene Dumas' work on paper, *Identity Crisis – Man Confusing Art and Life* from 1993 shows a man with a huge erect penis. His erection rises up and has his white belly as its background. The belly looks like a sheet of paper, and the penis like a brush that is going to leave its traces on it. The man looks down at his erection as if not knowing what to do with it or about it. A text on the top of this image says 'Identity crisis?' and that is exactly what his face seems to express. The 'confusion of art and life' of the title is then the reason for this possible identity crisis. Is his erection the inclination for creativity or for procreation: is procreation creative, like making a drawing or painting? Or should sexual pleasure not be confused with either of them? Whatever the answer is, the man does not seem to be at ease with his proud erection. He feels rather alienated, yes: ashamed of it. His sexuality is certainly not the foundation of his masculinity, but rather the embarrassing and shameful undermining of it.[10]

The two other ink drawings by Dumas have equally telling titles. The first one is titled *Two Bearded Beauties* and the second *Beauty as Burden*. Each image shows two standing nudes with very long hair, comparable to some of the Magdalene paintings she made in the same period. The women in *Two Bearded Beauties* are shown frontally; in *Beauty as Burden* we see one from the back, the other frontally. All four women wear a grim expression, as if they are angry. The long hair of the left woman in *Two Bearded Beauties* reaching almost to the ground; it looks as if she has a bat in her hand. This impression adds to their angry stance: she is going to beat. The face of the left woman is also very dark, almost black, and she has dark red, almost bloodshot eyes. And, as the title of the other image already suggests, the women in this image have beards. Their angry look is emphasized, perhaps motivated by the attribute or 'prop' signifying masculinity, namely their beards.

It is clear that the beauty of these four women is not a burden, because they are not ashamed of their beauty, or the lack of it. They bestow shame on the onlookers, on us, the viewers of Dumas' images. In that sense, these two images can be compared to the painting *Olympia* by Manet, already discussed, which created such a scandal in Paris in the salon of 1865, by confronting the public with her stern,

Ernst van Alphen

almost angry or contemptuous look. Her beauty was also clearly a burden to her, according to Manet. By returning the voyeuristic look of the viewers in the salon, the audience could do only one thing: redirect or refocus their gaze shamefully.

The images of Polish artist Artur Żmijewski relate to those of Natasja Kensmil and Marlene Dumas by showing gestures of contempt, hatred, and exclusion. They express the hate-speech slogan 'Shame on you!' in the most explicit way. Żmijewski has taken these photographs using the classic technique of chronophotography, which captures human movement through multiple exposure. We know this kind photography especially from nineteenth-century photographers like Étienne-Jules Marey. Each of Żmijewski's images is a study of a specific confrontation aimed at the viewer. Instead of recording actual public scenes, Żmijewski has them enacted in a studio using professional actors, thus neither analyzing the roots of the violence nor ascribing them to any particular identity. He looks at the gestures themselves and their morphology, beyond context or ideology. A range of aggressive gestures becomes a synthesis of behaviours.

Those behaviours exist as a means of expression both in private and public spaces where they constitute social relationships based on domination and exclusion. Taking the moment when Żmijewski made these images into consideration, namely 2019, two more specific contexts for the slogan 'Shame on you!' impose themselves. First of all, the international outcry against sexual abuse and intimidation of the Me Too movement; secondly the Polish

Artur Żmijewski, *Gestures*, 2019, chronophotography

context of an extreme right-wing government. Those two together suggest that the object on which shame is bestowed in Żmijewski's images, is male sexuality and male authority, both abusive. It is of course also the context of this itinerary through art that activates these two elements of masculinity as objects of shame on top of, but also through that framing, the two historical contexts.

The three animations of 2020 by Indian artist Nalini Malani, were specially made for the exhibition 'Shame! and Masculinity' that took place at H401 in Amsterdam. They do not address the issue of 'Shame on you!' beyond context or ideology, but from an Indian perspective, where prime minister Narendra Modi has been remaking India into an authoritarian Hindu nationalist state. Reports of extremely violent rapes, often by groups of men, have come not only from South Africa, but especially from India, in recent years. This suggests that it is not just male authority, but also male sexuality (and often the one enforced by the other) that is at stake in this country and deserves the outcry 'Shame on you!'

Malani has been making animations since the sixties, but only she started making iPad animations since 2017. These latest animations she describes as 'thought bubbles' or 'memory emotions'. When she sees or reads something that captures her imagination, she reacts by making a drawing or drawings in motion. The animations are thoughts and fantasies 'shouting from the head'. These thoughts and fantasies are not necessarily stemming from the same person or voice; hence, each voice gets a different penmanship.

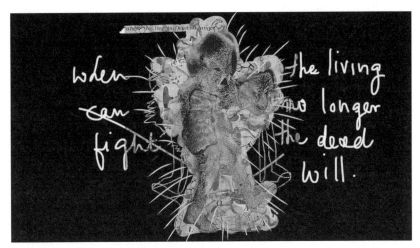

Nalini Malani, *Rebellion* (still), 2020, animation

The mood and the visual language of the recent iPad animations differ from the earlier animations by having a sense of the abject: they are funny, sad, energetic, hysterical and acute, and genre-wise, at the same time absurd, comical and satirical. By being abject, Malani's memory emotions try to expel that what is only too familiar to her as an Indian female artist: male sexuality enforced by male authority.[11] The first animation entitled *The Rebellion of the Dead Will Be the War of the Landscapes* is inspired by the play *The Task* by Heiner Müller from 1979. It is about the rape of the landscape, as a metaphor for quarrying and thus destroying the forest lands of the tribals by crony capitalists who are supported by the Indian government. Images and texts go by so fast that it is difficult to really see and read them. Afterwards one is not really sure if one has seen what one has seen. The modality of looking at Malani's animation is highly significant. Although the depicted scenes happen regularly in India (but not only there), we are not really aware of what happens. And like the others, the animation is very short: it is over before one has been able to start focusing on it. Ontologically, her animations are like unconscious images that only enter the mind in the form of nightmares, which are gone the moment one awakens. Her animations require the kind of attention that one needs for remembering a bad dream: that is difficult, not only because it was a dream, but also it was a dream one wants to forget.

The second animation *Workers* is, at first sight, only about male authority, not about male sexuality. It depicts the aggression of an upper-class despot against the working class. The so-called despot is a creature with two feet and two heads, and looks like a hairy reptile or caterpillar. The form and look of this little monster evoke rather negative notions of male sexuality; it is more than just an image of a patriarchal figure, for it connects the authority of the patriarch to his sexuality. This figure suggests that male authority and male sexuality are not separate issues, but are intimately related. Perhaps also that male authority is fuelled by male sexuality and that male sexuality as such is 'overpowering' and authoritarian. Leo Bersani has called this notion of authority a 'phallicizing of the ego' that is reflected in a practice of male sexuality as 'self-hyperbole'.[12]

11. Nalini Malani, *Can You Hear Me?* (Mumbai: Goethe Institut/Max Mueller Bhavan Mumbai, 2019), p. 12.

12. Leo Bersani, 'Is the Rectum a Grave?', in *Aids: Cultural Analysis, Cultural Activism*, ed. Douglas Crimp (Cambridge, MA: MIT Press, 1988), pp. 197–222.

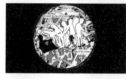

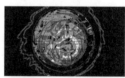

Nalini Malani, *Workers*, 2020, animation

The sequence of images is again extremely fast, as if to suggest that these insights are too unacceptable to enter our mind and to reflect on. The third animation Asifa refers to the Kathua rape case. Asifa Bano was an eight-year old girl who was abducted, raped, and murdered in the village of Rasana near Kathua in Jammu and Kashmir. This extreme sexual violence was ethnic cleansing in the form of rape. Male sexuality was used to perform a political act.

The three animations show different manifestations of a phallicizing of the ego. As a result, rape, exploitation of workers, and acts of ethnic cleansing become similar because they are all forms of abuse, resulting from a sexualized notion of authority.

Non-phallic Masculinity

As argued before, in visual culture the shameful sexuality of men can be dealt with in two ways. First, by denying shame and showing no signs of any awareness of their sexuality; second, by refusing any representations of shameful male sexuality in the visual domain. The first option was chosen in the (neo)classical, whereas the second option became prevalent in the nineteenth and twentieth centuries. But of course, especially in the domain of art, there are examples of male nudes, especially from the Renaissance period, that go beyond these two options. Michelangelo's *Dying Slave*, made between 1513 and 1516, now in the collection of the Louvre, shows the nearly naked body of a young man. His rather small genitals seem at first sight to be an example of unawareness of his sexuality, but this reading is countered by the expression of the rest of his body. Although euphemistically titled the *Dying Slave*, one may wonder what kind of death is at stake here: the so-called 'small death' experienced after sexual pleasure, or physical death? In any case, it is clear that the eroticism of this male nude is not at all phallicized. His penis, like his body, is vulnerable, and from a phallicizing perspective it is also shameful.

Another example is Caravaggio's Cupid as Victor, made in 1601, now in Berlin. The depiction of this young man, representing Cupid (!), is highly sexual but in no

Michelangelo, *Dying Slave*, 1513–1516

Ernst van Alphen

respect at all phallic. There is also no shame for male sexuality involved in this kind of representation, nor lack of awareness of sexuality. The boy confronts the gaze of the viewer self-confidently and 'victoriously'. Caravaggio's painting *St. John the Baptist* (1602) is another example of non-phallic masculinity. These Caravaggio paintings seem to imply that male sexuality is only shameful when phallic. Other kinds of male sexualities can be exposed freely, without being shameful or shameless.

These three images and the artists who made them belong, of course, to the homoerotic canon. This could suggest that homoerotic images escape the specific, intimate connection between shame and masculinity. Or that they overcome it through being more shameless. I refrain from answering such unwarranted generalizations, but I offer these possibilities for reflection. Instead, in what follows I will pay special attention to the healing role of shameless-ness in the overcoming of shame.

The male nudes by American artist Alice Neel, however, do not belong to the homoerotic canon, but rather to a feminist one. Here too, shame does not seem to be an issue, nor shamelessness. The painting *Joe Gould* from 1933 is, in a double sense, modelled on the idea of the Holy Trinity, in a double respect, but it is not obvious if that means the Father, the Son, and the Holy Ghost. Three male nudes are symmetrically posing next to each other, but the middle one is sitting and has three penises and six balls. It is more evident to understand the Holy Trinity as referring to the penis flanked by two balls at each side.

Michelangelo Merisa da Caravaggio, *Cupid as Victor*, 1601

Michelangelo Merisa da Caravaggio, *St. John the Baptist*, 1602

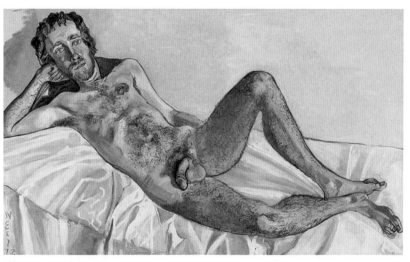

Alice Neel, *John Perreault*, 1972

And this trinity is repeated three times on the centre male nude who addresses the viewer with his penetrating gaze. *Joe Gould* seems to be an ironic comment on a very famous sculpture of the goddess of fertility, *Ephesian Artemis*. This goddess of fertility has many breasts, although some have argued that the breasts are in fact bull testicles. Whatever they are, it clearly signifies an excess of fertility. Although the figure of Joe Gould is turned into an erotic embodiment of fertility, he is not phallic. His fertility is not so much assigned to his penis, but to the flanking balls. Also, Neel's later male nude *John Perreault* of 1972 is not at all phallic and also emphasizes the testicles rather than the penis. The rest of this male body does not radiate male power in whatever way either.

Alice Neel, *Joe Gould*, 1933

The American artist Barkley L. Hendricks parodies the racist attribution of phallic masculinity to black men. According to racist conviction, all black men are endowed with a big, indeed enormous penis. The anxiety of white men that their wives will enjoy a black lover more than their white husband is visualized in the sight of a phallic monster or penis. When Hendricks had an exhibition in 1977, it was positively reviewed by the white art critic Hilton Kramer. He described the artist as 'a brilliantly endowed painter'. As a response Hendricks depicted himself in the nude with a self-assured gaze confronting the viewer in the painting titled *Brilliantly Endowed (Self-Portrait)*. In fact, he depicted himself not completely naked, but with some athletic attributes signifying machismo. But the centre of attention is his thumb slightly elevating his penis so that it will demonstrate his special 'endowment'. But as we all know, the size of the penis is relative; according to the stereotype this penis is enormous, but is it? What we see is a black male body, but how phallic it is remains the question. The attributes are tongue-in-cheek artificial additions to the body, in order to mislead viewers of the Hilton Kramer kind, who are misled by stereotypes.

Ephesian Artemis, date unknown

Overcoming Shame

As already explained, shame isolates. Because the relationality with the other person is broken or no longer

Barkley L. Hendricks, *Brilliantly Endowed (Self-Portrait)*, 1977

Ernst van Alphen

under control, a painful individuation is the outcome. The symptoms of the fallen face and blushing skin indicate the trouble felt when a circuit of communication is broken, and at the same time a desire emerges to reconstitute the interpersonal link. In this section I will deal with three artists whose work can be seen as attempts to overcome the isolation as a result of shame. This is relevant, because shame is a process that goes in two directions: it isolates, and this isolation asks to be worked through and overcome.

The first two artists are both South-African/Dutch, namely Ina van Zyl and Marlene Dumas. The third is Dutch sculptor Hans Hovy. Van Zyl's work is, as she says herself, 'grounded in shame'. Many of Van Zyl's (self)-portraits show a fallen face, as do, metaphorically, her depictions of the South-African flower, the Skaamrosie.

Another characteristic of her work is the sheen on the skin of the figures she paints. This sheen evokes issues of pride, dignity, self-display, and even exhibitionism. The sheen suggests the pride of the glossiness that covers the objects as well as the paint. This pride is so outspoken that it suggests to be the effect of an overcoming of shame through these varied behaviours. But it is not only the sheen that has this effect. Her zooming in and blowing up are rather uninhibited and shameless. It is the artist who is shameless in her deployment of devices to obtain images. There is no modesty in how she relates to what her eye has chosen for depiction. This shamelessness becomes visible because she leaves no distance. But, secondly and in tension with this, the resulting image can be considered shameful. The body parts do not relate or communicate any longer with the rest of the body. The link between object and context—in other words, detail and whole—has been broken. The body parts are no longer *part* of anything; in their isolation, they have become autonomous.

This autonomy is ambivalent and rather fright-ening, because it is symptomatic of a failure to relate. At the same time, the autonomy signifies a contextual isola-tion. Through a combination of shameless depiction and shame-inducing isolation, both shamelessness and shame are activated in these images. They seem to shape each other; they relate to each other in the most intimate way. In an interview with Dominic van den Boogerd,

Ina van Zyl, *Skaamrosie*, 2007, oil on linen, 50 x 40 cm

AMBIVALENCE

SHAME! and Masculinity

13. Dominic van den Boogerd, 'Blushing Muse: Ina van Zyl in conversation with Dominic van den Boogerd', (trans. Beth O'Brien in *Ina van Zyl: Schilderijen, aquarellen / Paintings, Water Colours* (Dordrecht: Dordrechts Museum; Bussum: Uitgeverij Toth, 2006), p. 19. A more elaborate version of my reading of Ina van Zyl's work can be found in *Highlighting Skin: Michael Kirkham and Ina van Zyl* (Schiedam: De Ketelfactory, 2020).

Van Zyl describes the role of shame in her work as follows:

> If you were to make a diagram of the layers in my work, then shame would be the bottom layer, the foundation on which everything rests and, at the same time, that which is hidden most deeply. I am not talking about a specific shame, but shame in general. Shame is not good or bad—I want to emphasize that ambiguity. Shame has to do with civilization. In other words, shamelessness, to me, is barbaric. The problem is: how do you paint shame? You could, for instance, paint a humiliating situation, such as the humiliation of prisoners in Abu Ghraib. Many artists do that. But that, for me is too illustrative. I have no desire to paint something that literal, and I am not interested in making paintings that have a message.[13]

According to this statement, Van Zyl's paintings are different from illustrative, literal paintings that have a message concerning shame. But they must refer to shame in order to avoid being 'barbaric' through their shamelessness and, instead, be 'civilized' through being grounded in shame. The second part of the passage concerns a problem of painting; the first explains the crucial nature of shame in culture.

Combining both aspects—the relation between shame and civilization, and that between shame and painting—this passage compels us to understand in what sense or under what conditions shame can attach itself to representation: how shame can intensify and alter the meaning of representation, and why that matters. The negation of shame is enacted in unfounded and unquestioned pride, dignity, self-display and exhibitionism. Together these feelings and acts demonstrate hubris. From the old-Greek noun *hybris*, the word means extreme pride, self-confidence, megalomania, brutality, and also shamelessness. In the Greek myths, humans are the ones who display hubris; they do not acknowledge their limited abilities compared to those of the gods. Icarus and Marsyas are humans who overestimate their capabilities. Their hubris is based on

Ina van Zyl, *Skaamrosie IV*, 2020, oil on linen, 60 x 45 cm

Ernst van Alphen

a technical practice or device: for Marsyas it was playing the flute, and for Icarus his artificial wings. Similarly, the practice of painting can be considered as hubris, because it is based on the act of creation, which cannot or may not be achieved by human beings. The Greek myths demonstrate this again and again.

Polish curator Adam Szymczyk explained the work of the artist Wilhelm Sasnal about the Polish involvement in the Holocaust as 'the desire to touch shame'.[14] The same can be said of Van Zyl's work, although the context that her work addresses is very different. Kasia Bojarska explains that by touching shame on a canvas or by an artistic practice one detaches oneself from a scene that was supposed to give pleasure. The two-directionality of shame is now articulated psychologically rather than socially. Eve Sedgwick and Adam Frank put it as follows:

> Only a scene that offers you enjoyment or engages your interest can make you blush. Similarly, only something you thought might delight or satisfy can disgust. Both these affects produce bodily knowledges: disgust, as spitting out bad-tasting food, recognizes the difference between inside and outside the body and what should not be let in; shame, as precarious hyperreflexivity of the surface of the body, can turn one inside out-or outside in.[15]

'Precarious hyperreflexivity' is exactly what paintings or other art practices that embody the desire to 'touch shame' bring about. Van Zyl's depictions of penises (and vaginas) touch shame by staging the duality of enjoyment and 'disgust'.

Van Zyl's assessment of shame and apartheid differentiates shame as producing isolated individuals from shamelessness as producing collectives. Skin colour was the principle on the basis of which this painful individuation and collective socialization took place. Under apartheid, shame attached itself to skin; it intensified and altered the meaning of skin in the most destructive ways.[16]

This political history of skin has fundamentally formed the painter Van Zyl. Over the years, her palette is more and more reduced to the darkest colours. As a result,

14. Szymczyk used this phrase in the conversation with Ulrich Loock. See *Sasnal Przwodnik Krytyki Politycznej*. Quoted in Kasia Bojarska, 'Wilhelm Sasnal's Transitional Images', Miejsce no. 6, 2020 (forthcoming).

15. Eve Kosofsky Sedgwick and Adam Frank, 'Shame in the Cybernetic Fold: Reading Silvan Tomkins', *Critical Inquiry* 21, no. 2 (Winter 1995), p. 520.

16. In the words of van Zyl: 'When I think of shame, I think of apartheid and the shamelessness with which the white South-African humiliated the non-white person. ... Shame isolates a person. When you have feelings of shame, you isolate yourself. It's something introvert; it separates you from others. With shamelessness, precisely the opposite takes place. People who humiliate others almost always do that in groups.' Van den Boogerd, 'Blushing Muse', p. 19.

Ina van Zyl, *Politician*, 2010, oil on linen, 70 x 60 cm

Ina van Zyl, *Stateswoman*, 2010, oil on linen, 55 x 50 cm

great portraits of, e.g. the Dutch King Willem-Alexander or Angela Merkel look as if they are 'coloured' persons. At first sight it seems that the brightness of white and of being white has become shameful. Is the dark palette the result of the taboo on white and on being white, as being shameful? I do not think so; it is more productive to see it as an homage to the colour that was shameful in Apartheid in South Africa until not so long ago. The dark skin of her paintings demonstrates that 'black is beautiful'. This political motto has become a painterly issue in Van Zyl's work. And as we have seen, the sheen on these dark skins, on the skin of the figure as well as the skin of paint, contribute to this pursuit of promoting blackness as the opposite of shamefulness.

Van Zyl's paintings are not literal or illustrative because they do not depict shame, nor racism for that matter, but enact the mechanisms of shame and shamelessness in their interrelationship. In her work, however, shamelessness is not overcoming or working through shame, as it would be in a proud portrayal of hubris. The reverse happens: shame is the enactment of overcoming the barbarism of shamelessness. Moreover, instead of representing that process itself, she starts a process that implicates the viewer. Inevitably, this implication is, in turn, grounded in shame. Hence the provocative subject matter of some of her paintings. Representations of vaginas and penises, the latter either erect or hanging, are still considered shameless. This is also why the glossy surfaces are both in the motif, for us to look at, and in the paint, which qualifies our way of looking at them.

If Van Zyl's work is grounded in shame, it means that it emerges from an inability to effectively arouse the other person's positive reactions to one's communications. Being a white South-African growing up under Apartheid, it is not surprising that her work is imbued with shame. Instead of ignoring or denying the political context that shaped her and her fellow South-Africans, Van Zyl's work is a self-reflexive renegotiation of the affect of shame that formed her. But as Sedgwick has explained, shame is not static; it directs itself at the same time towards a restoration of that sociability. The fact that Van Zyl became an artist shamelessly enlarging body parts, demonstrates her effort to restore sociability by means of painting. But although grounded in shame, it does not mean that her work is exclusively focusing on masculinity. But still, many of her works are devoted to male issues. For instance, she has shamelessly painted penises in all kind of shapes and conditions. Of course, she has also painted a number of vaginas, from different viewpoints and distances. But the fact that those have often metaphorical titles like 'Landscape', suggests that those depictions are less shameless; they are not thrown in the face as literally as the penises are, because they lend themselves to figurative readings. The fact that penises impose themselves visually, sexually and from time to time aggressively, makes them shameful and shameless at the same time.

Van Zyl's varied depictions of shame, like her 'Skaamrosies', but also her depictions of erect or hanging penises, are shameless as depiction, because of the way she paints these subjects. Her zooming in on body parts and other objects exhibits them as autonomous beings. Her shameless depiction of masculinity, or better 'male conditions' is a way of facing shameful masculinity. By facing it, she overcomes its shamefulness, so that we can again enjoy

Ina van Zyl, *Lul*, 2010, oil on linen, 60 x 40 cm

Ina van Zyl, *Enlarged*, 2017, oil on linen, 90 x 45 cm

the touching visibility of a penis, either erect or hanging. An early painting shows shameful masculinity in the most quintessential way. For nothing is more shameful for a man than when he cannot get an erection when he would like to have one, or the other way around: when he happens to get an erection, when it is not at all intended, or better, not welcome. The erection in *Big Man* is the most literal manifestation of the isolation of a man by shame.

Painting the Penis

Van Zyl's artistic project to overcome shame has resulted in a great number of depictions of penises, hanging, but most of the time erect. Especially the erections raise the question of how it is possible that the depiction of an erect penis is able to work through shame? Is the shameless exposure of this male condition already enough to neutralize the shame produced by male authoritarian behaviour? How does this work? During her artistic career, Marlene Dumas has also developed a special commitment to depict penises. The title of one such depictions makes clear what the problem is when one yields to this artistic challenge. The title is *The Making of Myths*. This ink drawing shows an erect penis from above as if focalized by its owner. The myth that originates here is the one that holds that he who possesses this penis is also in possession of the phallus. The phallus is a symbol, a very privileged one, and should not be confused with the male body part. As a symbol, the phallus stands for power and control, for a specific notion of subjectivity that can be best understood as a phallicized ego. Women can also be phallic, in possession of this power, but according to the myth, exclusively beings in possession of a penis are in possession of the phallus. In other words, the myth conflates the penis with the phallus, and by doing so it naturalizes the politics of patriarchy.

The ink drawing *Quicksilver* shows an erect penis from above as if focalized by its owner. The title indicates the illusionary nature of the conflation of an erect penis with the phallus: the penis is like quicksilver and has no stable form.

Ina van Zyl, *Big Man*, 2003, oil on linen, 160 x 80 cm

Marlene Dumas, *The Making of Myths*, c. 1998, ink, ink wash and acrylic on paper, 50 x 35 cm

Ernst van Alphen

It is telling that two artists who are women, Van Zyl and Dumas, have the ambition to depict male members that do not give rise to the suggestion that penis and phallus are the same. Then, even the erect penis is nothing but a special condition of a male body part. Van Zyl's zooming in and cropping of male (but also female) genitalia, isolates these body parts from the subjects who own them. The fragmented bodies do no longer enable viewers to read these body parts as symbolic; they are just body parts. The titles of two of Van Zyl's erect penises are utterly literal: *Dick By Dawn* and *Circumcised*. There is no suggestion of Phallic power any more. Van Zyl's painting *Two is Company* is also significant: it shows the hand of a woman holding an erect penis. But who or what has, or owns power and control in this image? The man, because his erection is supposed to symbolize the phallus? Or the woman's hand, which is clearly in charge?

Dumas' drawing *A Fragile Male Object* shows a soft penis; its title is again telling. First of all, it is 'a' male object; it is not 'THE' male object. It is comparable to other body parts; hence, it is no longer the origin of myth. It resonates with Michelangelo's *Dying Slave* by showing the male penis (and body in Michelangelo's case) as fragile instead of phallic.

The titles of the two works *Soft Focus* and *Distorted Image* are ambiguous and seem to say something about the image as well as about what we see depicted in the image. *Soft Focus* is an ink drawing and the spreading ink, indeed, creates an image in soft focus. But the soft-focus

Ina van Zyl, *Dick By Dawn*, 2009, oil on linen, 60 x 50 cm

Ina van Zyl, *Two is Company*, 2004, oil on linen, 65 x 65 cm

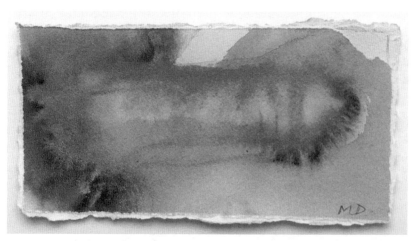

Marlene Dumas, *Quicksilver*, 1999, ink wash and acrylic on paper, 10 x 21 cm

technique often used in erotic photography with artistic ambitions, like the work of David Hamilton, shows a soft penis, which still should get some focus to become erect. Dumas' *Distorted Image* shows a penis that is distorted in many ways. It is not really clear whether it is erect or not; this distorts its symbolic power. Its Phallic potency is undermined by the ambiguity of the image.

Dumas' peace monument *Sketch for a Monument of the Peace/Watercolor with Sculptural Pretenses* from 1993 consists of two sheets with each two human figures adoring a huge soft penis, one hanging down, the other lying flat. The figures adore the penises as if they were the Golden Calf. Because these penises are not phallic, they can function as peace monument; there is no power or male authority involved, only a touching male body part. Although extremely funny, the repercussions of this 'sketch for a peace monument' are 'monumental', because of its deconstruction of the interconnection between male sexuality and male power or authority. The result is adorable.

The drawn penises of Arnoud Holleman's *Family and Friends* (2002) are cute too. The title of these drawings does not emphasize phallic competition (who has the biggest one, which one is the biggest), but presents these different sizes and shapes as being related or as variations of sameness.

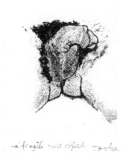

Marlene Dumas, *A Fragile Male Object*, 1984, ink and crayon on paper, 29.5 x 21 cm

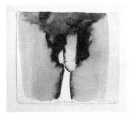

Marlene Dumas, *Soft Focus*, 1993, ink and ink wash on paper 26.5 x 30.5 cm

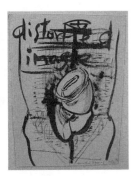

Marlene Dumas, *Distorted Image*, 1987, ink and crayon on paper, 31 x 23 cm

Marlene Dumas, *Sketch for a Monument of the Peace/Watercolor with Sculptural Pretenses*, 1993, ink wash on paper two parts, 18.5 x 18 cm and 19 x 18.5 cm

Formless Sexuality

So far, the presentation of artists and their work in this essay follows an itinerary from anger about shamelessness, especially male behaviour towards attempts to overcome the isolation of shame, to something else; an alternative, a non-phallic masculinity. So, this itinerary has to end with a positive closure: with the sculpture of Dutch artist Hans Hovy. His works are rather suggestive by showing a profusion of male and female genitalia, of sexual positions and acts. But it is difficult to disentangle them, to understand which body part is what and belongs to whom. It is also important that his works do not contain clear-cut, literal representations of body parts; they are just suggestive, which implies that as body parts they only exist in the eye of the beholder.

Hans Hovy, *White Beauty*, 2010

At first sight, Hovy's works bring to mind some sculptures Louise Bourgeois made in the sixties, especially *Homage to Bernini* (1967), *Janus in Leather Jacket* (1968), *Janus Fleuri* (1968), *Fillette* (1968) and *Cumul 1* (1969). Her *Homage to Bernini* literalizes the inner, bodily experiences at stake in the most famous sculptures of the virtuoso sculptor Gian Lorenzo Bernini; these are white marble masterpieces with great erotic resonances. The *Ecstasy of Saint Teresa* (1647–1652) and *The Ecstasy of Blessed Ludovica Albertoni*

Hans Hovy, *Sodom*, 2006

Hans Hovy, *Gomorra*, 2006

Gian Lorenzo Bernini, *The Ecstasy of Blessed Ludovica Albertoni*, 1674

Gian Lorenzo Bernini,
St Sebastian, 1617

(1671–1674) show most emphatically bodily, sexual ecstasy, whatever the religious or mythical pretext of the stories is. The blessed Ludovica touches her breast in rapture, which is demonstrated by her open mouth. Bernini's sculpture of St. Sebastian too resonates with sexual meanings. Of course, the depiction of this male saint has been part of a long tradition in which his body pierced by arrows has been taken as a pretext for representing, and looking at, a beautiful male body. In the case of Bernini's sculptures, it is, however, not just the viewers who enjoy these bodies, but also the sculpted figures themselves who do so. The St. Sebastian by Bernini's assistant Antonio Giorgetti is another case in which the death of St. Sebastian is ambiguous, for suggesting the 'small death' of ejaculation, instead of his physical death.

Bourgeois' bronze homage to this canonical sculptor displaces the erotic affect and meaning of Bernini's sculptures from the skin of the figures to the inner space of an abstract volume. Whereas (neo)classical sculpture depends for its outer appearance on an inner 'essence' or feeling that shows itself on the skin and outer appearance, Bourgeois shows an inner, bodily space that is not responsible for the outer appearance of the bronze object. Bernini's inner, bodily experience expressed on the skin by gestures, becomes in Bourgeois' work a literal inner space, like a secret world in the body. This inner space can also be recognized in many of Hovy's sculptures; in his case too it can be seen as a reconfiguration of the body. No longer an inner essence or feeling that becomes visible as outer appearance, but an exploration of the body as having inner spaces, literally. Eroticism does not only manifest itself on the skin, but also in the inner worlds of the body.

Although inner spaces of the body are conventionally seen as characteristic of the female body, male bodies also have them. It is remarkable that Bourgeois' *Homage to Bernini* is ambiguous in not specifying this bodily object as male or female. This is also the case in her white marble sculpture *Cumulus 1*. The bulging round objects are very suggestive, connoting both male and female body parts. The same can be said of her work from 1984 titled *Blind Man's Buff*; although the title of this work suggests otherwise, its appearance is far from convincingly male.

Louise Bourgeois, *Homage to Bernini*, 1967

Louise Bourgeois, *Cumulus 1*, 1969

Louise Bourgeois, *Blind Man's Buff*, 1984

Ernst van Alphen

61

This ambiguity is also typical of Hovy's work; although his works show inner spaces and protruding, phallic forms, it is too easy to see them as referring to the female and male body. And if we read the protruding forms as little penises, then it is clearly not signifying a phallic masculinity.

Bourgeois' ironic work *Fillette* transforms the supreme phallic object, a big erect penis into just a penis. First of all, this is done by the title *Fillette*, meaning little girl.[17] Second, by hanging the penis on a hook, as if a slaughtered ox, this phallus is shown after the act of castration. Robert Mapplethorpe's well-known photograph of a smiling Louise Bourgeois carrying the 'little girl' under her arm foregrounds Bourgeois' ironic appropriation of the mythical question of who owns the phallus and who does not?

Elsewhere I have argued that Hovy's sculpture is comparable to that of Giacometti, especially from the latter's surrealist period, because the works of both artists do not consist of a body on a console or plinth, but of scenes of several elements on a platform.[18] But while the surrealist-erotic platform scenes of Giacometti assume the gruesome forms of a battlefield, those of Hovy are chiefly playful and light-hearted, despite ironic designations such as *The World of Sodom and Gomorra*. His platforms are not battlefields but playgrounds. With Hovy, the scenes are about innocent and naive children who unsuspectingly, and without any awareness of the implications of sexuality, stick their penises or fingers in every orifice, or present their vulvas, mouths or anus to anyone who asks. In an age dominated by sexual intimidation issues, this portrayal of sexuality is not only literal and emphatic; it is also liberating. For sexuality is not only dead seriousness. In the history of art Giacometti's battle fields are rather common: according to most mythical and biblical stories sexual relations are violent and even deadly. Hovey's playgrounds show another image of sexuality, an image that is rather provocative after the recent years of Me Too conflicts. His scenes of sexual encounters, whatever the nature of these encounters is, are not at all battlefields. They rather look enjoyable, pleasurable, yes, even arcadian; a playing field rather than a battle field.

17. See for a brilliant reading of these Bourgeois works in relation to her so-called cells and spiders: Mieke Bal, *Louise Bourgeois' Spider: The Architecture of Art-Writing* (Chicago, IL: University of Chicago Press, 2001).

18. 'Scenes from a Marriage', in *Hans Hovy: King of Sculpture* (Amsterdam: Onrust, 2019), pp. 8–41.

Louise Bourgeois, *Fillette*, 1968

Robert Mapplethorpe, Louise Bourgeois, 1982 (carrying her own sculpture *Fillette*, meaning little girl)

Hovy's idyllic depiction of sexuality should not be regarded as a naive idealization. The scenic depiction of sexuality as a battlefield is more common, as we see, for example, with Giacometti, and for that reason Hovy's playing fields are more provocative. Or perhaps we should say that Hovy's depiction of sexuality is provocative precisely because it is a naive idealization. This is inevitable, because ever since Adam and Eve were banished from paradise, sexuality has lost its innocence once and for all. Nonetheless, some of Hovy's sexual playing fields have titles such as *Total Innocence or Small, Little, Lovely*. With these works and their titles, the distinction between good and evil seems to be ignored or even actively denied. Whereas Adam and Eve become aware of their sexuality outside of paradise and cover themselves in shame, Hovy's works seem to express no sense of shame whatsoever. This is rather a matter of uninhibited surrender. The form of sexuality that is being evoked here can be called, following Sigmund Freud, polymorphous, and this in the most literal sense. It concerns forms that, no matter how they are, can merge effortlessly with one another. One of the consequences of this is the fluidity of all associations; in other words, there are no fixed meanings to be ascribed to these forms. Male, female, top or bottom, all fixed positions and roles are inverted or interchangeable. The many inner spaces shown in Hovy's works are no longer typically female, nor can the protrusions be considered typically male. All his bodies have inner spaces and bulges and can be called polymorphous. This turns masculinity literally inside out. Male bodies are no longer defined and determined as being phallic and aggressive, but by a fluid and sensual interaction of inner and outer spaces. No reason to be ashamed anymore.

FLUIDITY

Hans Hovy, *Inside Beauty,*
2009/2010/2013

Hans Hovy, *Small Sodom,*
2007/2008/2013/2020

Ernst van Alphen

PAINTING A NAKED MAN
VOYEURISM
PRIVATE PARTS

Marlene Dumas

Painting a Naked Man

I have drawn many things, but I have
not made a painting of a naked man
more than once, well, twice, the first
embarrassed attempt was in 1975.
The title of the painting done in 1987
is *The Particularity of Nakedness*. The
title was inspired by the re-reading of
John Berger's *Ways of Seeing* (1972), in
which he draws a distinction between
the 'nude' and the 'naked' in European
oil painting. At art school in the 1970s
it was clear that no-one was inspired
by the nude drawing classes anymore.
The women (of colour) who posed
at the university had been there for
many many years. Being a model had
become their occupation. They had
posed themselves into (still-life-like)
generalized objects, devoid of erotic
(or any kind of) energy. The rare
occasions that the male nude (white)
was acquired, it led to giggles or
indifference but not to concentration.
Now it seems that it was not the nude

I was looking for, nor the posing figure,
but the erotic conditions of life that I
was after. Two 'subjects' confronting
each other. 'Apart from the necessity
of transcending the single instant and
of admitting subjectivity, there is, as
we have seen, one further element
which is essential for any great sexual
image of the naked. This is the element
of banality, which must be undisguised
but not chilling. It is this, which
distinguishes between voyeur and
lover. Here such banality is to be found
in Rubens's compulsive painting of the
fat softness of Hélène Fourment's flesh
which continually breaks every conven-
tion of form and (to him) continually
offers the promise of her extraordinary
particularity'.*

As we move from the *Specific*
to the *Type* we come to:

Voyeurism

Why do my pictures escape the 'voyeuristic gaze'. This was a question put to me recently. My reaction was: I'm not a Peeping Tom, I'm a painter, I'm not even a photographer. But I think the answer is in the J. Berger quote above. The aim is to 're-veal', not to 'display'. It is the discourse of the Lover. I am intimately involved with my subject matter in this painting. I am not disengaged from the subject of my gaze. With photographic activities it is possible that they who take the picture leave no traces of their presence, and are absent from the pictures. Paintings exist as the traces of their makers and by the grace of these traces. You can't TAKE a painting— you MAKE a painting.

Private Parts

Some comments from my viewers on the painting *The Particularity of Nakedness:* A woman (writer) told me she was very disappointed in seeing this work, she used to enjoy my older, more conceptional work, so much but what was I doing now—painting pictures for gay men. She called it a homosexual painting?! She said my male was too passive. Will we ever get beyond the hetero/homo dualism? A man (museum director) told me that the painting was a failure due to too many horizontals. It was apparently very hard to paint a good painting without any vertical elements. Just recently I saw that John Baldessari did a work *Horizontal Men* (1984). He said it was the obverse of a man vertical, the measure of things. It was a vulnerable alternative. I liked that. The difficulties with this work made me think of the depictions of the sexual organs of Christ (remember *The Sexuality of Christ?***) although somehow in the reverse. My male image was experienced as 'not strong enough'. Both parties wanted him erected one way or another.

*
John Berger, *Ways of Seeing* (London: Penguin Books, 1972).

**
Leo Steinberg, *The Sexuality of Christ in Renaissance Art and in Modern Oblivion* (London: Faber, 1983).

These three texts were originally written in c. 1991.

Reissued with the kind permission of Marlene Dumas. Originally published in *Miss Interpreted: Marlene Dumas* (Eindhoven: Stedelijk Van Abbemuseum, 1992), pp. 26–80; and included in Marlene Dumas, *Sweet Nothings: Notes and Texts*, ed. Mariska van den Berg (2nd rev. and exp. edition London: Koenig Books, 2014), pp. 62–63.

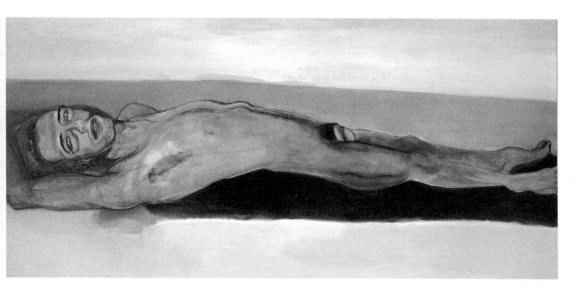

The Particularity of Nakedness, 1987
oil on canvas, 140 x 300 cm

Marlene Dumas

NATASJA
KENSMIL

Untitled, 2004
drawing, charcoal on paper, 150 x 150 cm

SHAME! and Masculinity

About 8 feet deep Saddam was found, 2004
drawing, charcoal on paper, 150 x 150 cm

Natasja Kensmil

Lynndie England III, 2005
drawing, charcoal on paper, 150 x 150 cm

SHAME! and Masculinity

Tsar Nicolas II (I hate you), 2004
drawing, charcoal on paper, 150 x 150 cm

Natasja Kensmil

Lynndie England II, 2005
drawing, charcoal on paper, 140 x 150 cm

The Birds, 2002
drawing, charcoal on paper, 94 x 150 cm

Creatio ex Nihilo, 2004
drawing, charcoal on paper, 151 x 150 cm

Natasja Kensmil

VIRILITY AND FASCISM

Lorenzo Benadusi

1. See Terry Kirk, 'Les lieux du stade: Fascisme et contrôle des corps', *Vacarme* 45 (Fall 2008), pp. 51–54; see also Carlo Cresti, 'Forum Beniti', *FMR* 26 (1984), pp. 102–111.

2. See Marcello Piacentini, 'Il Foro Mussolini in Roma, arch. Enrico Del Debbio', *Architettura e arti decorative* 2 (February 1933), p. 74; Mario Paniconi, 'Criteri informativi e dati sul Foro Mussolini', *Architettura* 2 (February 1933), pp. 76–89.

3. Mario Morandi, 'Il Foro Mussolini', *Critica fascista* 7 (1934), p. 651.

The statues in the Stadio dei Marmi in Rome's Foro Italico furnish an example of the image of the ideal Fascist man. With their 'virile and chaste nudity' they were meant to create such a visual effect as to condition the young athletes of the Farnesina and to promote their acquisition of a masculine identity.[1] According to Marcello Piacentini, the new architectural complex was endowed with 'the features of eternal Rome' and offered 'a picture of Hellenic beauty', while Mario Pancioni saw the Foro as 'almost like an anthem to Fascism, a solemn celebration of eternal Italic youth and vigour, which this youth has regimented, organized, and revived, to steer it toward its most elevated, inevitable destiny'.[2] The 60 statues, which came from all of Italy's provinces, were 'spectacles of virile—and at the same time grandiose—beauty' that provoked 'solemn and heroic thoughts'.[3] The fascination of Fascism was based in part on this image of the young and virile man, an image that was idealized but was so attractive precisely because

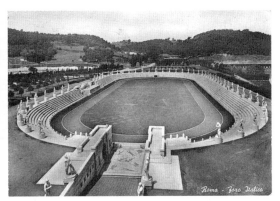

Stadio dei Marmi, Rome

Stadio dei Marmi, Rome, statues

of that idealization.[4] However, this bodily representation of the ideal Fascist man scarcely corresponded to the actual physical build of Italians: these Herculean marble sculptures were greatly different from many Fascists, who were scrawny, short, and little accustomed to sport. Sironi emphasized how unrealistic the artistic representation of the male body had always been: 'Michelangelo's *David*, at which, it seems, stones were thrown in his day, is so polished and gigantic as to be an extravagance, Cellini's *Perseus*, with his biceps inflated like tires and with so much bronze-work spread across his body … is abnormal, excessive, unusual, strange.'[5] The Fascist representation of a male youth, marching in uniform, acted as a counterpart to this other Italian, who was tired, weak, and emaciated from poverty and hard work. Even among the images at the Istituto Luce one finds many more traces of farmers and members of the petite bourgeoisie than the new strong and virile man promoted by Fascism. And even documentaries of the day continued 'to show a pacific and industrious Italy, peace-loving, bourgeois, without conflicts or irrational outbursts'[6]: an Italy, in short, that was more prosaic and rural than heroic and martial.

The relationship between masculinity and Fascism seems obvious at first glance. The regime rendered this link self-evident, conveying an image of itself centred on virile ardour and the martial force of men in black shirts. Owing above all to the development of gender studies and men's studies, the relationship between masculinity and Fascism recently has become an object of historiographical analysis. Nevertheless, contemporary historiographical scholarship on Fascism and questions of gender has added little to our understanding of the characteristics of the martial, virile Fascist male, often embellishing, with rhetoric and too much psychoanalysis, an existing and well-known description. In particular, some Anglo-Saxon scholars have overly embraced a cultural approach that is too attentive to language and representations.[7] These studies have paid particular attention to the literary and artistic production of intellectuals and have often read the provocations of the avant-garde movements too literally, imagining Fascist masculinity as a sort of incarnation of the super male theorized by F.T. Marinetti: seducer, rapist, and untiring lover.[8]

4. On the fascination of Fascism, especially in terms of the male image, see Susan Sontag, *Sotto il segno di Saturno* (Turin: Einaudi, 1997); and Jeffrey T. Schnapp, 'Fascinating Fascism', *Journal of Contemporary History* 2 (1996), pp. 235–244.

5. Mario Sironi, 'Mal sottile', *La Rivista illustrata del popolo d'Italia* June 1934, pp. 23–32.

6. Gabriele D'Autilia, 'Il fascismo senza passione: L'Istituto Luce', in *L'Italia del Novecento: Le fotografie e la storia*, vol. 1, *Il potere da Giolitti a Mussolini, 1900–1945* (Turin: Einaudi, 2005), p. 111.

7. John Champagne, *Aesthetic Modernism and Masculinity in Fascist Italy* (New York: Routledge, 2013), p. 4.

8. On the relationship between Futurist and Fascist virility, see Barbara Spackman, *Fascist Virilities: Rhetoric, Ideology, and Social Fantasy in Italy* (Minneapolis: University of Minnesota Press, 1996).

VIGOUR

9. Robert Connell, *Mascolinità, identità e trasformazioni del maschio occidentale* (Milan: Feltrinelli, 1996). On the concept of hegemonic masculinity, see Nikki Wedgwood, 'Connell's Theory of Masculinity: Its Origins and Influences on the Study of Gender', *Journal of Gender Studies* 4 (December 2009), pp. 329–339; Demetrakis Demetriou, 'Connell's Concept of Hegemonic Masculinity: A Critique', *Theory and Society* 3 (June 2001), pp. 337–361; Jeff Hearn, 'From Hegemonic Masculinity to the Hegemony of Men', *Feminist Theory* 1 (January 2004), pp. 49–72; Simonetta Piccone Stella, 'Due studiosi della mascolinità a confronto: Pierre Bourdieu e Robert Connell', in *La costruzione dell'identità maschile nell'età moderna e contemporanea*, ed. Angiolina Arru (Rome: Biblink, 2001), pp. 89–96. For a new clarification of the concept of masculine hegemony, see Reawyn Connell (the female name, after a sex change, of Robert Connell) and James Messerschmidt, 'Hegemonic Masculinity: Rethinking the Concept', *Gender & Society* 6 (December 2005), pp. 829–859; and R. Connell, *Questioni di genere* (Bologna: Il Mulino, 2006).

10. Alberto M. Banti, *L'onore della nazione. Identità sessuali e violenza nel nazionalismo europeo dal XVIII secolo alla Grande Guerra* (Turin: Einaudi, 2005).

11. Klaus Theweleit, *Male Fantasies* (Minneapolis: University of Minnesota Press, 1987–1989); Jonathan Littell, *Le sec et l'humide: Une brève incursion en territoire fasciste* (Paris: Gallimard, 2008).

Scholars thus often end up describing the ideal of masculinity rather than its real expression, more the fantasies than actual realizations. Virility tends to seem a discursive and symbolic invention, devoid of any link with actual male self-perception. The concept of hegemonic masculinity—developed, using a definition of hegemony in the Gramscian tradition, by the Australian sociologist Robert Connell—or rather a connotation of man that is hyper-virile, traditional, misogynist, homophobic, and aggressive, that stigmatizes any different form of self-expression, refers to an ideal type that is valid more as an ideal model than as a realistic example.[9]

Such an approach also overemphasizes the aspects of continuity linked to gender identity. The problem is not due so much to the use of the *longue durée* as an instrument of analysis. Instead, the concept of virility—interpreted simply as honour, courage, violence, and sacrifice in defence of the homeland and the family—is abstracted from individual historical contexts, tending to appear the same in every geographical setting, unchanged over time. This happens, for example, in Alberto Mario Banti's studies on gender in the canon of the Risorgimento, in which the virile ideal passes unchanged in a continuous thread from the French Revolution to the Risorgimento, from the Great War to Fascism.[10] The risk of this approach is not being able to grasp the particularities of single moments and privileging continuity over breaks and permanence over change. This risk is also present in studies that are more attentive to the psychological dynamics inherent to masculinity; I am referring in particular to research on the mass psychology of Fascism, which considered Fascism to be the result of the authoritarian and reactionary psychology expressed by a bourgeois, sexually repressed male. I am thinking, for example, of the works of Theweleit and Littell on the male fantasies of the *Freikorps* or of German soldiers deployed in the Russian campaign. In these studies, Fascism is born from the need of the male soldier to equip himself with a body that he has transformed into muscular armour, into a kind of cuirass to defend himself from every possible external contamination.[11] In short, Fascism was born from the attempt to give order to a disordered world, where impulses and emotions risk calling into question traditional masculinity. Here again fantasies and desires are prevalent, while, in my opinion, moving beyond this discourse and focusing on behaviours and identities can better help us to advance our historical understanding of the relationship between Fascism and masculinity.

War, Postwar, and *Squadrismo*

Demonstrating virility meant above all being ready to fight for the homeland, donning the uniform to distinguish oneself even at the cost of one's own life. The Great War has been analyzed in light of these aspects and was viewed as a conflict that tested the virility of youths eager to become real men. The effects of life in the trenches and of direct contact with death remain, however, more ambiguous than they appear at first sight. On closer view, 'hegemonic masculinity' emerges from the war both reinforced in its aggressive elements and weakened by the danger of moving towards a gradual emasculation and dangerous depletion of pre-war martial heroism.[12] The view of the First World War, upheld by historiography, as stimulating and fortifying stereotypical male attributes and reinforcing the nexus between masculinity and militarism, does not, however, take into account how the war experience caused soldiers to perceive their own diminished virility and the fragility of their bodies. In some cases, it was the harshness of life at the front that softened the virile traits of the combatants, as Piero Calamandrei confided to his girlfriend:

> They say that war renders one, physically and morally, more masculinely crude and insensitive: I find in myself, however, at least as far as morale is concerned, that each day of this absurd life that passes my soul becomes more and more open, almost femininely, to every incitement toward softening.[13]

First to be challenged was the distinction of gender roles, as demonstrated emblematically by the instance of artillery Sergeant Ottone Costantini and war pen pal (*madrina di*

12. On the coexistence of both traditional and transgressive masculine traits during the war, and on the transformation of virility, see Jason Crouthamel, *An Intimate History of the Front: Masculinity, Sexuality, and German Soldiers in the First World War* (New York: Palgrave Macmillan, 2014); Joanna Bourke, *Dismembering the Male: Men's Bodies, Britain and the Great War* (London: Reaktion, 1996); Kate Hunter, 'More than an Archive of War Intimacy and Manliness in the Letters of a Great War Soldier to the Woman He Loved, 1915–1919', *Gender & History* 2 (2013), pp. 339–354; Anthony Fletcher, 'Patriotism, the Great War and the Decline of Victorian Manliness', *History: The Journal of the Historical Association* (January 2014), pp. 40–72.

13. Letter of 22 July 1916, in Piero Calamandrei, *Zona di guerra: Lettere, scritti e discorsi, 1915–1924* (Rome and Bari: Laterza, 2006), p. 96.

14. Ottone's letter to Sandra of 12 May 1917, in Claudio Costantini, ed., *Un contabile alla guerra: Dall'epistolario del sergente di artiglieria Ottone Costantini (1915–1918)* (Turin: Paravia, 1996), p. 130.

15. Letter of 18 September 1915, in ibid., p. 86. On soldiers' crying and other bodily manifestations of their emotions, see André Loez, 'Tears in the Trenches: A History if Emotions and the Experience of War', in *Uncovered Fields Perspectives in First World War Studies*, ed. Jenny Macleod and Pierre Purseigle (Boston: Brill, 2004), pp. 211–266.

16. Letter of 26 June 1917, in Costantini, *Un contabile alla guerra*, p. 141.

17. Letter of 25 October 1917, quoted in Antonio Gibelli, *La guerra grande: Storie di gente comune, 1914–1919* (Rome: Laterza, 2014), p. 143.

HEROISM

guerra) Sandra Andenna, two lovers who married at the end of the conflict. Their relationship began with all the rituals of bourgeois respectability: first, they had to overcome the difficulty of informing their families of their relationship, a difficulty generated by an upbringing that, founded on strictness, coldness, and modesty, had 'impeded emotional expression and thus reciprocal intimacy'.[14] Further, they tried to conform themselves to established gender ideals: the woman who ennobles the man, preventing him from transforming into a brute 'with an embittered soul', and the virile man who fights without complaining, and stifles his tears 'because [they are] not very warlike'.[15] Little by little both began to move toward an inversion of roles. Ottone, due directly to his relationship with Sandra, discovered with astonishment that he preferred domestic intimacy to war, as he explained to her:

> I once felt that I was destined to wander the earth toward the novel, the adventurous, the exciting, in feverish activity, in keeping with my aspirations. And today my inclinations have all changed! Two years of emotions and exhausting efforts, and a sweet voice coming from the marvellous Roman sky, have extracted the insanity from my heart, replacing callous restlessness with a strong feeling of desire and affection. Now I too am looking for my peaceful nest, hidden beneath a roof overlooked by everyone, like that of my little swallows, which I have left to their happy fate. I want joy, rest, and, above all, love. I want to drown in an ocean of love.[16]

Sandra's path, however, was the opposite, as she was overcome with patriotism and intoxicated by the heroism of her boyfriend, wanting to give up her peaceful life and dress like a man to take part in the conflict. At this point her womanhood was holding her back, and she confessed to feeling the weight of her 'weak sex' that caused her to envy Ottone and all of his 'bold companions'.[17] After the defeat of Caporetto her desire to make herself useful to the *patria* was even stronger, and with a firm and decisive tone she wrote:

I envy you, I envy you! ... Don't talk to me about too much enthusiasm and recklessness or I will get very upset this time! ... A few times I tried to study the way to become a little soldier ... but there's too much indecency! ... To be discovered and put in all the newspapers is a type of publicity I've always avoided![18]

18. Letter of 27 October 1917, quoted in ibid., p. 144.

19. Letter of 8 December 1917, quoted in ibid., p. 146.

20. Letter of 16 December 1917, in Costantini, *Un contabile alla guerra*, pp. 212–213.

With even more insistence she continued to make clear to her companion her refusal of that 'troublesome quality of women who can't follow the path of duty and vengeance!'[19] This non-acceptance of her own womanhood, combined with an all-encompassing passion for the nation, annoyed her beloved artilleryman, who with this earnest letter tried to re-establish the 'correct' division of gender roles, curbing his girlfriend's heroic passions:

> My dear little Sandra, wouldn't it seem more rational to you for a woman to passively accept her destiny ... lightening our sacrifice with a little of that selfish, saintly love that is family affection? Isn't this more noble and holy than the other?! ... Why invert the order established by nature and by God at such an inconvenient time? If you only knew how lovely is that saintly woman, free of heroic sentimentality, who lends a tone of sadness to every sentence that mentions the slaughter of humanity! Nor have I heard many of these lovely phrases from you! Why, then, let yourself be led, because of a noble feeling of scorn, to forget, or at least, to misinterpret your very important mission, which is that of all women? Believe it! The example of the Spartan mothers (if they even existed!) isn't meant for our civilization.[20]

Antonio Gibelli correctly points out how in the private sphere of this romantic relationship are reflected 'the dilemmas of an encounter-clash between genders which runs through the entire history of the war'; in fact, Ottone was forced to admit the 'curbing of that virility' that the conflict should have enhanced instead:

21. Letter of 21 June 1918, quoted in Gibelli, *La guerra grande*, pp. 148–149.

22. See Paola Di Cori, 'Il doppio sguardo: Visibilità dei generi sessuali nella rappresentazione fotografica (1908–1918)', in *La Grande Guerra: Esperienza, memoria, immagini*, ed. Diego Leoni and Camillo Zadra (Bologna: Il Mulino, 1986), pp. 765–799.

23. See Ana Carden-Coyne, *Reconstructing the Body: Classicism, Modernism, and the First World War* (Oxford and New York: Oxford University Press, 2009).

24. Barbara Bracco, *La patria ferita: I corpi dei soldati italiani e la Grande Guerra* (Florence: Giunti, 2012), p. 224.

My dear little Sandra, to call it a torrent of sadness, a whirlwind of ill humour, would not be enough to fully describe my mood in this moment. … I am experiencing the desolate isolation of a lost man, forgotten, indifferent to everyone. If I had to describe my feelings in symbols I would draw an infinite, oppressive series of perfect circles, decentred, and large and small, intersecting, where the eye is unable to find relief in a straight line, and the mind is forced to whirl around in a thousand turns. It is a tiresome turmoil, a physical depression.[21]

Ottone thus made a painful confession that clearly demonstrates the gradual deterioration of the soldier's martial image, with the resulting risk of beginning a process of feminization and infantilization.[22] The trauma of the war created anxieties and fears—all clear signs of weakness—and even a new way of experiencing emotions. These could include loss of self-control, cowardice, panic, and terror, which inevitably called into question the hyper-virile model of the officer grounded in stoicism and heroism. The wounded, maimed, and disabled took on even more clearly feminine traits: passivity, dependence on others (almost always women), vulnerability, feminine aptitudes and duties such as sewing, gardening, the weaving of wicker baskets, and regression into an infantile state, demonstrated by pleasure in holding a teddy bear or by employment in the production of toys. It was chiefly the loss of mobility, strength, and action, all essential traits for a soldier, which created a terrible shock and a problematic relationship with one's own gender identity.[23] The attempt to erase this image of impotence and insufficient virility—caused by the absence of the male traits of knowing how to work and to fight—began with the use of prostheses and cosmetic surgery, diminishing the disfiguring effects of wounds to the body or to the face, and above all with the glorification of heroic, wounded figures. The first such figure to be celebrated in magazines and newspapers as 'a champion of warlike virility' was Enrico Toti who, disabled in a work accident, managed to recover his status as a valiant fighting man at the front, brandishing his crutch against the enemy.[24]

Behind the rhetoric of the wounded soldier as a symbol for the wounded homeland in its rightful aspirations was concealed the often much sadder reality of the war-wounded. Resented by society, soldiers faced difficulties that society attempted to resolve through welfare and charity. War wounds also signalled a destabilized masculinity, since only rarely was a wound, like a virile tattoo, seen as a symbol of heroism; much more often it was seen as an irreversible disfigurement or mutilation. Disability suffered in war could also affect emotional bonds, as is clear from the words of the writer Elio Bartolini: 'Tobia was destined to become his son-in-law, had he not lost an arm on the Carso: and of this wounded man, even with a pension, my aunt Giulia, his lover, no longer wanted anything to do with him.'[25]

The war seemed to have undermined the foundation of the archetype of virility, showing the fragility of its ideal expression: the male warrior. In the trenches, young men in the prime of their strength experienced exhaustion and physical deterioration, but above all they saw the principal masculine qualities put to the test: courage, sense of duty, self-control, and self-discipline. Thus, it was no longer an age of heroes, since in the face of the total arbitrariness of death, almost any chance to present oneself as a valiant soldier vanished. In short, if success in combat no longer depended on individual merit, but rather on fortune or fate, then military virtues were no longer linked to virile ardour, but to the capacity to endure and to obey. Historians have begun therefore to focus on the emasculating effects of the conflict, considering the Great War as the moment of crisis of the 'virile-military' nexus.[26] In the end, there were too many expectations placed upon men to be able to overcome the trials of war. The code of masculinity was so centred on courage and the capacity to fight that it provoked grave concerns about not being able to live up to it. Elaine Showalter has shown, for example, how shell shock represented a form of escape from this overly rigid model of virility.[27] Since men could not show themselves to be weak and vulnerable, then to express fear meant to refuse more or less consciously not only war but also the very idea of masculinity. Even camaraderie had a double valence. On the one hand, it allowed soldiers to experience corporeality

25. Elio Bartolini, *L'infanzia furlana* (Treviso: Santi Quaranta, 1998), p. 61.

26. See Stéphane Audoin-Rouzeau, 'La Grande Guerre et l'histoire de la virilité', in *Le triomphe de la virilité Le 19 siècle*, vol. 2, *Historie de la virilité*, ed. Alain Corbin (Paris: Seuil, 2011), pp. 403–411.

27. Elain Showalter, 'Rivers and Sassoon: The Inscription of Male Gender Anxieties', in *Behind the Lines: Gender and the Two World Wars*, ed. Margaret Randolph Higonnet et al. (New Haven: Yale University Press, 1987), pp. 61–69.

28. Crouthamel, *An Intimate History of the Front*, p. 8; see also Thomas Kühne, 'Comradeship: Gender Confusion and Gender Order in the German Military, 1918–1945', in *Home/Front: The Military, War, and Gender in Twentieth Century Germany*, ed. Karen Hagemann and Stefanie Schüler- Springorum (Oxford and New York: Berg, 2002), pp. 233–254.

29. Eve Kosofsky Sedgwick, *Between Men: English Literature and Male Homo-social Desire* (New York: Columbia University Press, 1985).

30. See Françoise Thébaud, 'La Grande Guerra: Età della donna o trionfo della differenza sessuale?', in *Storia delle donne: Il Novecento*, ed. Georges Duby and Michelle Perrot (Rome and Bari: Laterza, 2003), pp. 25–90; Michela De Giorgio, 'Dalla "Donna Nuova" alla donna della "nuova Italia"', in *La Grande Guerra*, ed. Leoni and Zadra, pp. 307–332; Rosella Prezzo, 'Il lavoro e la guerra', *Italia contemporanea* 180 (September 1990), pp. 547–552.

31. Jean-Yves Le Naour, '"Il faut sauver notre pantalon": La Premiére Guerre mondiale et le sentiment masculin d'inversion du rapport de domination', *Cahiers d'histoire Revue d'histoire critique* 84 (2001), p. 44.

32. On this topic, Sandro Bellassai's interpretation of fascist masculinity as a restoration of a traditional and anti-modern virility is not entirely convincing, considering that the glorification of an aggressive and martial virility is also present in movements like Futurism that explicitly refer to modernity and are not at all reactionary or anti-modern Bellassai, *L'invenzione della virilità: Politica e immaginario maschile nell'Italia contemporanea* (Rome: Carocci, 2011).

33. For some critical observations on this thesis, see Lorenzo Benadusi, 'Borghesi in Uniform: Masculinity, Militarism, and the Brutalization of Politics from World War I to the Rise of Fascism', in *In the Society of Fascists: Acclamation, Acquiescence and Agency in Mussolini's Italy*, ed. Giulia Albanese and Roberta Pergher (New York: Palgrave Macmillan, 2012), pp. 29–48; Lorenzo Benadusi, 'A Fully Furnished House: The History of Masculinity', in *George L. Mosse's Italy: Interpretation, Reception, and Intellectual Heritage*, ed. Lorenzo Benadusi and Giorgo Caravale (New York: Palgrave Macmillan, 2014), pp. 29–46.

in a collective environment, reaffirming their own gender through rapport with others of the same sex; on the other hand, soldiers 'created an imaginary universe where they could temporarily live with the idea of going outside the norms of masculinity, experimenting with "feminine" emotions', without wanting to destroy traditional gender dichotomies.[28] From this perspective, it is significant that an institution like the army, completely centred on relationships among men, adopted the most repressive means when confronted with the erotic expressions of these relationships, supporting Eve Kosofsky Sedgwick's thesis of the existence of an interdependence between 'homosocial desire' and 'homosexual panic'.[29]

The last challenge to masculinity came from the transformation of gender roles, due to the greater freedom experienced by women in the absence of their husbands. The new female role came to be perceived by veterans as a threat, and the greater public visibility of women, who were becoming more and more active, scared men, who were determined to defend their predominance at any cost.[30] The traumas caused by years spent at the front led to a need to reinforce traditional masculinity; because of this defensive reaction, 'the fragility of men ended up paradoxically reinforcing the virile ideal'.[31]

This aspiration toward an authoritative restoration of masculinity in an anti-modern key has been considered by historians as one cause of the rise and success of Fascism.[32] Using George L. Mosse's reflections on war as brutalization, Fascism has been understood as a movement intent on emphasizing the violent and hyper-virile traits of the soldiers in grey-green. Fascism, then, is interpreted here as a response to the crisis of masculinity, in order to maintain warlike conditions during peacetime and to militarize Italians with a view to new battles.[33]

With the birth of *squadrismo*, the organization of the Fascist militia-party was meant to create an armed phalanx based on the virile daring of young men, united by camaraderie and by a shared faith in an ideology.[34] The rites and symbols of the Blackshirts were based on myths of conquest and the glorification of regenerative violence. Through a warlike aesthetic, they were meant to imbue a hyper-virile temperament into the male body. From this perspective, the political juxtaposition with rivals took on an anthropological connotation, which made the body of the enemy the symbol of irreconcilable difference among contrasting types of humans (thin/fat; soldier/non-soldier; young/old; active/inactive; virile/effeminate; strong/weak; and healthy/sickly). Even the young Communists of the 'Ordine Nuovo' opposed the old sterile and impotent reformism, hoping for the recruitment of a 'mighty proletarian army', formed by a 'mass as numerous as possible of well-built and developed men, ... balanced in harmonious development in all parts of their bodies'.[35] After all, if it was a matter of civil war from both sides, it was necessary to have members capable of fighting it; but from this perspective Fascism could count on veterans and their younger brothers, determined to demonstrate that they were capable of bravely facing the enemy within. The whole universe of bravery, built on violence, fearlessness, hatred of the quiet life, and glorification of unbridled virility both martial and sexual, came together in the *fasci di combattimento*. Ferruccio Vecchi's *arditismo civile* was also 'a true kind of sexual bravery', imbued with Futurism and D'Annunzianism, in which for men everything was permitted and everything was licit.[36]

The virile characteristics of *squadrismo*, its military camaraderie, its display of force, and its capacity to glorify the masculinity of its members have been closely analyzed by historians who have emphasized its total challenge to bourgeois respectability, which was based on self-control, temperance, and the preservation of good manners.[37] The young *squadristi* rejected not only the socialists but also all the 'conformist petit bourgeois'. Little by little, the *squadristi* felt the great distance that separated them from the 'upright people' and even their own relatives.

> I realize that I am, or rather that we are, changing [wrote Mario Piazzesi in his diary]. We have become hard, rude, always irritated, with a colourful, but very popular style of speech. My mother thinks that we are hardening our spirits, we who talk of guns, who remember past conflicts, and who hope for new ones insistently, as if this were the only purpose of our lives.[38]

34. See the contribution by Matteo Millan in this volume.

35. Caesar, 'L'esercito socialista: Educazione e disciplina', *L'Ordine Nuovo* 11 (October 1919), pp. 164–165.

36. Quoted in Giulia Belletti and Saturno Carnoli, *L'ardito: Vita provocatoria di Ferruccio Vecchi* (Ravenna: Edizioni Moderna, 2013), p. 57.

37. Sven Reichardt, *Camicie nere, camicie brune: Milizie fasciste in Italia e in Germania* (Bologna: Il Mulino, 2009); Cristina Baldassini, 'Fascismo e memoria: L'autorappresentazione dello squadrismo', *Contemporanea* 3 (July 2002), pp. 475–505; Emilio Gentile, *Storia del partito fascista 1919–1922: Movimento e milizia* (Rome and Bari: Laterza, 1989); Mimmo Franzinelli, *Squadristi: Protagonisti e tecniche della violenza fascista, 1919–1922* (Milan: Mondadori, 2003); Matteo Millan, *Squadrismo e squadristi nella dittatura fascista* (Rome: Viella, 2014).

38. Mario Piazzesi, *Diario di uno squadrista toscano, 1919–1922* (Rome: Bonacci, 1980), p. 166.

Squadrismo at the Stadio dei Marmi, Rome, between 1932–1939

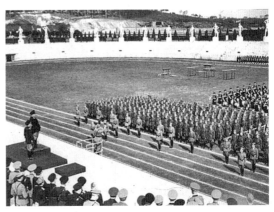

Military parade at the Stadio dei Marmi in Rome in front of Benito Mussolini, between 1932–1939

39. Marcello Gallian, *Il soldato postumo Romanzo* (Milan: Bompiani, 1935), pp. 64–65.

In their eyes, 'bourgeois' was synonymous with cowardly, and the struggle against 'anti-national' forces took on the contours of a no-holds-barred fight to assert one's virility at the expense of that of the enemy, who was forced to surrender because of his lack of it. In fact, in the account of Marcello Gallian, it was not men but women—the wives of the Communists—who thrashed the Fascist martyrs like beasts. Dragging him, they had almost stripped him, and the women had to tear him from the hands of the men. They all scratched him, tore out his hair, enjoying it as if he were their own rebellious son, from their own womb: then they grabbed him. 'Not dead, no, but you must return to your mother disfigured', and, crazed, they began to squeeze where a man shows himself to a woman, when they are alone. Gustavo struggled, his eyes bulging— 'Don't maim me, don't maim me, kill me instead.' When they had covered him with hateful spit and scratches and bite marks, they abandoned him and he began to run, crying: he cried not because of the blows he had taken, but because they had disfigured him in that place that is the source of man's pride at being born different from woman: and so, feeling sorry for himself, he walked.[39]

Contrary to what Klaus Theweleit has argued, even though the Fascist man lived in a state of perpetual war, where the essence of virility derived from courage and heroism, wartime experiences did not inevitably brutalize the servicemen. Only a relatively few among them (the Italian *arditi* or the German *Freikorps*) continued to use violence. Moreover, if during the 20-year span of Fascism, the *squadrista* apostle-warrior became a model of the new man, at the same time, for the regime, this model risked appearing somewhat excessive, with his overtones of anarchic individualism, heroic volunteerism, intimations of an aristocracy of combatants or a caste of the elect based not on lineage but on courage, the unrestrained expression of violence, and masculinity. Not coincidentally, then, immediately after the seizure of power, Fascist representations of the *squadristi* tended to downplay their aggressive and martial traits, portraying them instead as elegant young dandies, occasionally even implying a hint of homosexuality.[40]

Loue, Sexuality, and Marriage

After rising to power, Fascism had to curb its original anti-conformist and rebellious tone in a difficult compromise between revolutionary thrusts and the maintenance of established order. In terms of virility, it was not easy to synthesize the ideal type of the strong and courageous warrior, thirsty for blood and in the grip of his own virile fervour, and that of the bourgeois who was frugal, hardworking, attentive to decorum, and in control of his passions. In short, on one side was a combative masculinity: heroic, martial, military, and violent; on the other was a disciplined masculinity: prosaic, domestic, civil, and peaceful.[41] This plurality of models obviously offers an interesting starting point for reflection, both on the difficulties encountered by Fascism in realizing the total politicization of existence and the total resolution of the private and the public. Fascism necessarily had to pragmatically and strategically calibrate its proposals for various audiences and different circumstances.

In any case, especially after Mussolini's 'Speech of the Ascension', the regime openly expressed its desire to give a political valence to private behaviour, trying to model masculinity, as well as femininity, on the needs of

40. See Enrico Sturani, 'Il fascismo in cartolina', in *Modernità totalitaria*, ed. Emilio Gentile (Rome and Bari: Laterza, 2008), pp. 113–117.

41. On the contrast and overlap between a domestic masculinity and a martial one, see Jessica Meyer, *Men of War: Masculinity and the First World War in Britain* (Basingstoke and New York: Palgrave Macmillan, 2011); for analogous conditions in the United States, see Amy S. Greenberg, *Manifest Manhood and the Antebellum American Empire* (Cambridge and New York: Cambridge University Press, 2005).

42. See Chiara Saraceno, 'Costruzione della maternità e della paternità', in *Il regime fascista: Storia e storiografia*, ed. Angelo Del Boca, Massimo Legnani, Mario G. Rossi (Rome and Bari: Laterza, 1995), pp. 475–497.

MACHO

43. Sharo Gambino, *Fischia il sasso* (Catanzaro: Edizioni Internazionali, 1974), p. 60.

44. See Alberto De' Stefani, 'L'obbligo del matrimonio e della filiazione', in *Commenti e discorsi* (Bologna: Zanichelli, 1938).

45. Luisa Passerini, *Torino operaia e fascismo: Una storia orale* (Rome and Bari: Laterza, 1984), p. 183.

the state.[42] From this perspective, the first priority was to favour demographic growth and to adapt moral tradition to Fascist ethics. Virility was to be demonstrated through the ability to reproduce and to fight. At the time, there was, in fact, a photomontage in circulation that featured twelve photographs of the same number of families, with the caption: 'Twelve wounded and 114 children—The war wounded in Italy certainly don't need demographic encouragement!'[43] Those who avoided their duty as soldiers, husbands, and fathers were obliged to pay the price for their shortcomings.[44] The attempt to invade the private life of individuals was enough to create resistance and a number of ploys to avoid such regimentation.

These non-conforming behaviours, while they cannot be automatically interpreted as conscious anti-Fascism, show the stubborn will of the population to adapt the rules imposed from on high to their own personal needs. The tax on unmarried men, for example, was seen as an intolerable political interference that could be avoided by claiming to be unemployed. The hostility towards a similar provision is shown in the words of Renzo Anselmo, a labourer from Turin interviewed by Luisa Passerini:

> A person at my workplace—the Fiat sawmill in Via Passo Buole—a person introduces himself to me and starts to say that they have given him a card to fill out to pay the bachelor tax, because in those days there was a bachelor tax, and men who weren't married after the age of 25 paid a tax. So this individual had already had six or seven operations. He was mutilated a little bit all over his body from it having been cut so much, and he complained, saying, 'It's a shame that I have to pay the bachelor tax. I won't ever marry because I'm not fit to be married or to support a family, or to even have one. On the contrary, it would be shameful for me to have a family in my condition.' And I say, 'You see how things are? We live in a world of theft, because if I want to get married, I'll get married, but if I don't want to get married I should have the freedom to do what I want, without paying a tax. This is highway robbery.'[45]

The bachelor tax, the impossibility of receiving career promotions without being a veteran, and even the risk of being subject to disciplinary measures for practicing sexual behaviours that did not conform to the norm all served to outline the ideal model of a man. Marriage loans and birth prizes, honours, and promotions, on the other hand, were useful incentives to induce citizens to conform to this model, which in many cases had already been internalized without the efforts of the party. The Church, with *Casti conubii*, advanced a family model centred on procreation within marriage, on opposition to abortion and contraceptive methods, on a hierarchic model of gender relations, and on the subordination of family members to the authority of the man, whom the woman 'was meant to serenely and nobly obey out of love, not obligation'.[46] The desire for discipline was also common, in this case exerted by priests charged with not allowing 'the faithful entrusted to them to err' and with keeping themselves immune from the 'pernicious doctrines' on contraception.[47]

Studies on the family under Fascism have widely shown the failure of the demographic policies promoted by the regime. Not only birth rates but also marriage rates offer evidence of the impossibility of imposing overly prescriptive behavioural models.[48] More than conformism and faith in ideology, there was the indifference of those who tried to keep politics out of the private sphere, as expressed in Alberto Moravia's literary representation of a bourgeoisie absorbed with its own individual drives and composed of 'stupid and small figures, hopelessly lost in the larger world'.[49]

Furthermore, tradition, customs, and established practices made changing behaviour extremely difficult, especially when it came to sexuality. Certainly, as far as masculinity was concerned, Fascism tended to reiterate and reinforce a virile model already largely established, legitimizing a chauvinism so intensified as to take on more and more pronounced characteristics of *machismo*. Marinetti's critique against romanticism, moonlight, and the *femme fatale* was revived, exalting the virile fervour of the man who loves passionately but without letting himself be carried away by sentimentalism.

46. Icilio Felici, *La famiglia: Sulle orme dell'enciclica 'Casto Connubi'* (Milan: Del Duca, 1938), p. 21.

47. Pio XI, *L'enciclica del s. Padre sul matrimonio cristiano: Per la resurrezione e la salvezza della famiglia* (Rome: Mondini, 1931), p. 20. See also Lucia Pozzi, 'Chiesa cattolica e sessualità coniugale: L'enciclica Casti connubi', *Contemporanea* 3 (July–September 2014), pp. 387–412.

48. Marzio Barbagli and David Kertzer, eds., *Storia della famiglia italiana 1750–1950* (Bologna: Il Mulino, 1992); Daniela Calanca, *Legami Relazioni familiari nel Novecento* (Bologna: Bononia University Press, 2004); Cecilia Dau Novelli, *Famiglia e modernizzazione in Italia tra le due guerre* (Rome: Studium, 1994); Paul Ginsborg, *Famiglia Novecento: Vita familiare, rivoluzione e dittature, 1900–1950* (Turin: Einaudi, 2013).

49. Alberto Moravia, *Gli indifferenti* (Milan: Bompiani, 1982 [1929]), p. 54; see also Alberto Moravia, *Se è questa la giovinezza vorrei che passasse presto: Lettere di amicizia, amore e formazione 1926–1940*, ed. Alessandra Grandelis (Milan: Bompiani, 2015).

50. Letter of Vittorio Palazzi to Lyda Iapoce, 3 January 1933, in Patrizia Salvetti, *L'amore ai tempi del fascio: Un carteggio (1932–1939)* (Cava de' Tirreni: Marlin, 2014), p. 151.

51. Letter of Vittorio to Lyda, 30 January 1938, in ibid., p. 250.

TABOOS

In this way, gender roles tended to become even more polarized, attributing languishing, sentimental feelings to women and uncontrollable passions to men. The correspondence between a young couple from Ancona clearly shows how these models were fully internalized. Faced with repeated refusals from his girlfriend, one young man wrote:

> You women think you will get a man's love by making him wait. You're wrong! Love today is a sickness that enters the bloodstream upon contact: the rest is romantic literature from the past, it's chatter, it's rhetoric, it can be at the most a side dish, but without sauce. … You are a woman, and being a woman, you are able to wait. But I, Lyda, am a man, and to be a man means to be a hunter, that is, to desire a woman, any woman.[50]

This virile audacity was more talk than reality. The same man ended up 'fighting against the body, against this base body' and little by little rejected 'the urges of the restless flesh', even considering premarital chastity a source of pride. Ultimately, he began to criticize the double standard and even to accept true gender equality:

> Man seeks absolute purity in a woman. Few men would keep the company of a woman who would give free rein to her presumed or actual sexual needs. With what spirit of justice and righteousness do we ask from others an act of will that we have not known how to or not been able to achieve ourselves? Here then is a criterion of basic honesty: either giving up feminine purity or giving up our relations until marriage.[51]

But it is above all the world of the farmer that shows itself to be impenetrable to the lifestyle changes imposed by Fascism. First we see the old habits, unchanged by time, and the deeply rooted taboos regarding sex that prevented men from having relations with women, if for no other cause than the rigid separation fixed by society: Sex.

In those days many young men were so timid that they were unable to even talk with a girl. ... Making love was difficult; the girls were not at all free like today. While out in the pasture one might say to a girl 'Do you need a labourer?' And if the daring proposal hit the target, so much the better.[52]

52. Testimony of Bernardino Gelleano, in Nuto Revelli, *Il mondo dei vinti: Testimonianze di vita contadina* (Turin: Einaudi, 1997), p. 57.

53. Nuto Revelli, *L'anello forte: La donna: Storie di vita contadina* (Turin: Einaudi, 1985), pp. 58–59.

The conditioning and restrictions imposed on women were much harsher:

Ah, sex was a sin. And even dancing was a sin. Those who went to church to confess and said that they went dancing would no longer be given absolution, no. ... We grew up without knowing anything about sex, or misunderstanding things. It's not true that we in the country understood because we were closer to nature. Yes, we saw the animals, but we didn't understand. We saw calves born, piglets. ... We saw animals coupling, but we didn't put it together that people were like this, never. I think that many marriages failed because we knew little or nothing. ... It was a mortal sin, it was scandal, an indecent thing, they raised us that way. The woman was rigid, restrained, tense as a wire, full of uneasiness, of fear. She experienced the sexual act as a scandal, not as a natural, spontaneous thing, and after a while the man got tired of it and went to look for sex from other women.[53]

This female rigidity, together with the potential of experiencing sexuality only with prostitutes before marriage, created a division between physical passion and emotions, constricting the emotional sphere. Male jealousy was born from this image of virility as uncontrollable sexual desire and from the idea that the glimpse of a woman was enough to drive a man to try to seduce her. There is record of a man who openly confessed to his girlfriend, 'I don't know why, but when I know that you're home, I'm happier and more relaxed'; one who made his girlfriend promise not to go down into the street; another who forbade her from 'sticking out [her] tongue' or laughing in public; one who forbade her from going to the beach in a swimsuit or

54. Letter of 26 February 1922, quoted in Antonietta Sammartano, '"Scrivimi, Anna mia, e a lungo, ti prego": Nino Sammartano to Anna Galli', in *Scrivere d'amore: Lettere di uomini e donne tra Cinque e Novecento*, ed. Manola Venzo (Rome: Viella, 2015), p. 227.

55. Vanna Piccini, *Nuove usanze per tutti* (Milan: Ed Mani di fata, 1938).

riding a bike in a skirt.[54] The code of honour was based on male control of the family's morality; fathers and brothers performed a close surveillance over women, rendering relationships between couples extremely cold and formal. In this arena, Fascism seems to have introduced some changes, since, as it favoured the participation of women in public life, it triggered some emancipatory processes, facilitating more free association among boys and girls. Even the waiting time before marriage tended to grow shorter, because, as Vanna Piccini noted in 1938:

> Long-term engagements, important to families at one time, don't work anymore. They were suitable in the days when it was required for the groom to have a solid position, and for the wife to have sewn with her own hands sixty dress shirts and thirty sets of bed sheets. Today, because the Regime, with the appropriate intentions, allows young people to provide for the wedding expenses, it is not only those who have a considerable estate who are allowed to set up house. Thus, brief engagements.[55]

Fascism pushed for a greater openness in sexual education in attempt to treat these subjects without bias or the influence of Christian doctrine. The fact that the call to have children had implicit libertarian valences that could conflict with bourgeois respectability and Catholic moralism is clearly evident in the directives issued to the perfect Fascist:

> There is nothing more thoughtless and ridiculous than that which is taught by certain jaundiced educators and certain seminaries, which we would venture to call dens of sudden, uncontrollable, sputtering urges toward ignominious homosexual masturbations; the sexual education in the *collegi*, both of males and females, leads to violent anxieties, crises of spirit, probable disgraces, gloomy doubts, and even the habit of lying. For males let the education be more frank, open, almost daring, and let it begin earlier. … This way we will have more men and fewer flirts, more seriousness and less shame, more loyalty and less pretence, and

more health: and most importantly, we will have the resulting Demographic Reawakening willed by the Sage Mind of the DUCE.[56]

From this hygienicist and natalist viewpoint, the regime's premarital 'certificate of health' was considered useful to provide the highest guarantee of the health of the future husband and wife. The proposal was opposed by the Catholics and by advocates for marriage as a spiritual tie that 'still rests upon a sufficiently moral foundation, despite illness, [because] the health of the body cannot be separated from the health of the spirit'.[57] Married life tended to alter gender relations; now it was up to the couple to take on—although with different roles—the management of the family, and in the case of working women, this could entail a redefinition of the figure of the head of household. In any case, the wife tended to transform herself little by little into a partner—into the confidante, the friend, the one who helps and supports. Of course, this all happened in the usual 'doll house' frame, but on closer view this gender imbalance was sometimes an expression of a female subjection more illusory than real. Even the choice of a partner was beginning to be more removed from the economic interests of the families, who, however, continued to have the last word on marriage proposals. One can see here the first signs of a challenge to the traditional role of the father and to the rigid patriarchal authoritarianism that prevented children from living their own emotional and sexual lives more freely. A generation accused of being too sanctimonious seemed incapable of grasping the changes caused more or less deliberately by Fascism. An adventurous spirit, dynamism, and fearlessness were all values that in some way challenged the bourgeois respectability of the oldest generation, who in fact tried to preserve the code of good manners by appealing to tradition.[58]

The persistence of this traditional ethos pushed the Italian population to refuse the antibourgeois campaign of the 1930s, which was viewed as undeserved meddling in private life. Despite public opposition, Fascism continued to press the issue of anthropological revolution, which shows that consensus was important but not essential.[59] The Italo-Ethiopian War generated a sincere enthusiasm

56. Ugo Giammarchi, *Stilizzazione Fasciste: Il galateo del prefetto Fascista* (Busto Arsizio: Pianezza, 1936), pp. 32–33.

57. Giuseppe Cattani, *Igiene del matrimonio* (Milan: Hoepli, 1929), p. 433.

58. See Gabriella Turnaturi, *Signori e signore d'Italia: Una storia delle buone maniere* (Milan: Feltrinelli, 2011).

59. See Simona Colarizi, *L'opinione degli italiani sotto il regime, 1929–1943* (Rome and Bari: Laterza, 2009).

Anti-Semitism in a leaflet: 'The Roman salute ...and this other one', n.d.

TIPI: NUMERO UNO

Different types of anti-Semitism, 'numero uno' type, n.d.

60. See Giulietta Stefani, *Colonia per maschi Italiani in Africa Orientale: Una storia di genere* (Verona: Ombre Corte, 2007); Cristiana Pipitone, 'Foto di gruppo Ritratto di ufficiali coloni', *I sentieri della ricerca* no. 7/8, 2008, pp. 183–204; Ruth Ben Ghiat, 'Unmaking the Fascist Man: Masculinity, Film and Transition from Dictatorship', *Journal of Modern Italian Studies* 10, no. 3 (September 2005), pp. 336–365.

61. Roberto Berardi, *Un balilla negli anni trenta: Vita di provincia dalla grande depressione alla guerra* (Cuneo: L'Arciere, 1994), p. 73.

62. Quoted in Paul Corner, 'L'opinione popolare e il tentativo di effettuare la militarizzazione della società italiana sotto il fascismo', in *Militarizzazione e nazionalizzazione nella storia d'Italia*, ed. Piero del Negro, Alessandra Staderini, and Nicola Labanca (Milan: Unicopli, 2005), p. 204.

and voluntary participation, particularly on the part of young men wanting to display their virile masculinity in the colony.[60] However, even militarism raised passions more performed than sincere, as would be shown tragically with the Italian intervention in the Second World War. The rigid repetitiveness, the exaggerated conformism, and the hierarchical order imposed by military training had already begun to feel tiresome to many young men; in fact, one former *balilla* from Fossano recalled, 'a certain displeasure began to spread among us adolescents for the incessant assemblies and parades, the stomping in the mud interspersed with long periods of dead time'.[61] The problem of a gradual rejection of training practices was perceived from on high, as can be seen from this report of the *federale* of Piacenza on the pre-military instruction of young men:

> The instruction takes place in total disorientation, the lack of discipline among the *premilitari* is due to the fact that they present themselves for training on Saturdays simply because they are threatened by disciplinary measures or by the resigned belief that otherwise they would be reported to the Military Authority for habitual unjustified absences. The young men show themselves to be lacking in enthusiasm and unprepared for the duties and obligations imposed by pre-military training.[62]

To all this was added the fact that now, facing a real war rather than a simulated one, in the moment when the public sphere most required individual sacrifice, private interests overwhelmingly won out. One young man recalled that the heroism of enlistment in the army was no match for the security of employment in a bank:

> You understand that I am giving up service so as not to lose the job at the Bank, seeing as my three months of probation have not yet passed. I don't know if you are happy with my decision, I found it to be right, being the most secure; the Bank of Italy for me means a career and a secure future. It means being able to marry you with confidence and in a short time to give you a safe and almost comfortable life. Right now this means everything

to me. Sure, for a young man military life, as an officer, is nicer, full of entertainment, satisfaction, etc., but for me none of this is appealing, my only goal is you, and it's only you that I want to join.[63]

63. Letter of Vittorio Palazzi to Lyda Iapoce, 21 July 1936, in Salvetti, *L'amore ai tempi del fascio*, p. 214.

64. Antonio Gibelli, *Il popolo bambino: Infanzia e nazione dalla Grande Guerra a Salò* (Turin: Einaudi, 2005).

65. Piero Girace, *Diario di uno squadrista* (Naples: Rispoli, 1939), p. 37.

This inability to take on such important responsibilities, as Gibelli has noted, was also due to the process of infantilization of the Italian population set into place by the regime in order to discipline them, make them obey unappealing commands, and to further tie them to the paternalistic bond with authority.[64]

Masculinity, the Fascination of the *Duce*, and Post-Fascism

Mussolini personified the complete realization of the figure of the masculine ideal. The appeal exuded by Mussolini was strong. His appeal had already been noted before he became the Duce of the Italian people. This carried weight especially with women but also with the many Fascist men who were seduced by his virile temperament and his statuesque physicality. The *squadrista* Piero Girace, for example, describes him thus:

> Although I looked at him and observed him at length—his bald, square-shaped head, his ample chest under the black shirt that, damp with sweat, clung to his skin, outlining his powerful torso— Mussolini to me was not a physical reality. He was one of those great characters that Tommaso Carlyle wrote about in his book *On Heroes*. ... 'The face of the Chief stiffened. It seemed to be made of stone. He didn't bat an eyelash. Silence fell; and this time it was a religious solemnness. I felt like I wasn't breathing. I didn't see anything but Him. And he abruptly began to speak.'[65]

The posture, the gaze, the bodily features, the solemn rhythmic gait, and the shrill voice, all emphasized the unbridled physicality of the Duce, whose charismatic power

UNISON

66. Quoted in Christopher Duggan, *Il popolo del duce: Storia emotiva dell'Italia fascista* (Rome and Bari: Laterza, 2012), 212; see also Camilla Cederna, ed., *Caro Duce: Lettere di donne italiane a Mussolini, 1922–1943* (Milan: Rizzoli, 1989).

67. Letter from Carlotta Ranocchia to Mussolini, 13 June 1932, quoted in Alberto Vacca, *Duce! Tu sei un Dio! Mussolini e il suo mito nelle lettere degli italiani* (Milan: Baldini & Castoldi, 2013), p. 79.

68. Ibid., p. 140.

was due in part to this expert performance of the characteristics of the superman.

Little by little, hero worship became a mass phenomenon in Italy through the figure of the Duce, while elsewhere it was tied more to movie actors or members of royal families. Women deified Mussolini to the point of transforming their adoration into attraction, as can be inferred from the many letters sent to him day after day from every corner of the country. The fascination was owed to the combination of normal, simple, and prosaic traits of the everyday man with the extraordinary characteristics of a unique figure, the unattainable hero, the uncommon person. In an exchange of views between two young women from Turin, both mentioned these aspects:

> I never saw him that way, I couldn't imagine him as a person to hug, to kiss: to me he was a god.
> – I don't know, I wouldn't know. … Yes, I like him, but as a lover …, I can't do it.
> – I like him as a man, too. He's very handsome, strong, dominating; I would like a man like that.
> – Her words seemed as decisive, as irrevocable, as mine were uncertain. Then there was the issue of age.
> – How old is he? I asked timidly.
> – I don't know for sure; but what does it matter? He's charming and healthy. I like him so much.
> I was still perplexed; I walked in silence while Fiorenza smiled, talking to me about him.[66]

The Duce's superman image reassured Italian men and women, giving them a sense of protection. They felt 'in unison, bound to Him with pure passion, and enthralled by His lofty virtues, [adoring him] as one honours a supernatural being, favoured by God who clearly protects Him and renders Him invulnerable in the face of most certain danger'.[67] A God, however, who was near to his people, and who they addressed in a friendly and direct way, as is clear in this letter sent by a young *balilla*: 'forgive me if I address you informally [with the *tu*], but even when I pray, speaking to God, I speak with such familiarity, because all of the Great are Good and indulgent'.[68] In short, there was the glorification of the figure of Mussolini, like a charismatic leader, a superman hero, a myth, and a living legend, but, at the same time, he was the ordinary Italian, the common man, who remained close to the people and embodied the model whom all were supposed to emulate.[69]

Mussolinism and the personalization of politics contributed both to the strength of Fascism and to its weakness. The intense hero worship risked provoking a counterproductive media overexposure, and the undisputed faith in the leader tied the fate of the regime exclusively to that of its head. As Sergio Luzzatto has pointed out, the body of the Duce, which from the beginning was a metaphor for the body politic, became, during the dramatic events of the civil war, the emblem of the nation's fate. The two images—one of the pale and sickly prisoner, freed by the Germans from the Campo Imperatore, and the other of the man hung upside down bare-chested from the scaffolding of a gas station in Piazzale Loreto, insulted by the crowd and mutilated by their blows—symbolized both the end of Fascism and, at the same time, the tragic consequences of an irrational exaltation of its figurehead.[70] According to Giorgio Fenoalta, only then was revealed the intrinsic weakness of the regime and its leader who 'was no more of a masculine leader than anyone else: on the contrary, he was a little less of one', because he hid his cowardly and feminine traits. Now your Duce, broad-chested and swaying, greedy for applause and admiration, fearful of personal danger, cowardly and at the same time cruel, was just like a woman: but his large, prominent jaw, to which physiognomists ascribe a particular meaning, was enough to excite the physical and psychic inferiority complex of a multitude of people, the description of which you will be able to find in any manual of psychoanalysis, and to earn them the reputation for strength that no one less than him deserved.[71]

During the purging process after Mussolini's death, the journalist Virgilio Lilli wrote that the Duce and his followers had physical and character traits that rendered them similar to women:

69. Stephen Gundle, Christopher Duggan, and Giuliana Pieri, 'The Cult of Mussolini in Twentieth-Century Italy', Modern Italy 18 (2013) 2, pp. 111–115.

70. See Sergio Luzzatto, Il corpo del duce: Un cadavere tra immaginazione, storia e memoria (Turin: Einaudi, 1998); and Sergio Luzzatto, L'immagine del duce: Mussolini nelle fotografie dell'Istituto Luce (Rome: Editori Riuniti, 2001).

71. Giorgio Fenoaltea, Sei tesi sulla guerra con note per i fascisti onesti (Florence: Barbèra, 1943), p. 39. On these aspects, see Lorenzo Benadusi, 'Women Don't Want Us Anymore' Militarism and Masculinity in the Italian War', in Lessons of War: Gender and the Second World War, ed. Corinna Peniston-Bird and Emma Vickers (New York: Palgrave Macmillan, forthcoming).

Actually [Giovanni] had always seen something feminine in all the expressions of both the leader and the men around him, almost as if they were girls who were playing at being men, and who as part of the game put all of their effort into form rather than substance, into the scowl, the tone; in short, into the costume or the theatre. In Mussolini, particularly in his crude and soft physique, he had often seen the features of a fat woman, a vain and restless woman, to be considered with a certain pity, if at all: and his love for uniforms, for ranks, for the court; that vanity comprised of the mirror, the tailor's scissors, the shimmering frills, the devotion to the scale as a weapon against one additional gram of flesh; even his military passion, all exterior, like that of a princess or a queen; ... that exquisitely feminine audacity with which he pronounced certain verdicts or covered himself with feather plumes or affected hard and furious facial expressions; yes, yes, that jutting out of the lip for photographs, that apprehension, that monitoring of photography, as is the custom of women who are always afraid of 'not looking good', disappointed if the photographer has 'fattened' or 'aged' them; ... all this enormous burden of femininity was unable to stir in Giovanni's soul any real suffering; on the contrary it created the surprising, and at the same

Military group, personal archive, n.d.

time ridiculous, spectacle of the woman in pants, fated to go down in history.[72]

72. Virgilio Lilli, *Una donna s'allontana* (Milan: Rizzoli, 1959), p. 34.

73. Indro Montanelli, *Ritratti* (Milan: Rizzoli, 2004), p. 363.

The fascists and Fascism were either too virile or not virile enough. The new republican Italy, having left behind the militarized virility of the fascist era, tried to recuperate the seductive virility of the Latin lover or the moderate virility of the Catholic and the good father. The change is evident in the juxtaposition of the figure of Mussolini with that of the new head of government, the Christian Democrat leader Alcide De Gasperi:

> From out of the shadows, the Italy of the lost war—writes Indro Montanelli— saw this unusual character emerge, and for this very reason maybe he reassured her much more than the gurus from before Fascism or the thundering tribunes like Nenni. De Gasperi was an anomaly. … An aura of cold air seemed to perpetually surround him. He was a man in grey, with grey, dry, unadorned oratory, with un-imperial grey eyes, with a face of stone, also grey. He was calm, patient, resistant to rhetoric and to ostentation. He was not a man of ideology, he was a man of ideals, which are two very different things. He was an unshakeable bourgeois, that one.[73]

This desire totally to transform individuals, which necessitated intrusion into the personal sphere—both public and private, physical and mental—was one of the basic characteristics of the totalitarian dimension of Fascism. The birth of the 'ethical state', where the moral and the political intermingled, led to increased social control of sexuality and more severe punishments for sexual behaviour that deviated from the 'normal'. As a result, to avoid the spreading of negative examples to the larger body, any violation of the established rules of virility led to expulsion from society. The homosexual was thus considered a dangerous disturbance to national order. Highly noticeable actions against individuals who brought into question Fascist virility with their 'filthy vice', however, held the risk of producing a negative effect, because they gave visibility to a social ill that damaged national honour and pride. Consequently, the repressive measures that were used varied according to circumstance and offenders were condemned through censorship, prison or isolation, exclusion or in the negation of homosexuality. To use one of Marcuse's categories, that which was defined as Italian Fascism's 'repressive tolerance' towards homosexuals was in fact an effort aimed at striking out at sexual 'anomalies', without publicizing the operations that were carried out to do so.

Fascist repression of homosexuals thus provides elements that are useful in defining the masculine canon the regime wanted to spread. Persecution focused almost exclusively on the effeminate, transvestites and prostitutes. From the Fascist point of view, homosexuality was not centred on an individual's sexual orientation. Paradoxically, the homosexual, defined as a person attracted to someone of the same sex, was relatively ignored. There were no specific books, discourse or measures taken regarding homosexuality per se because only the absence of virility was a problem. A sedentary middle-class man, an English dandy or an elegant refined Parisian represented negative symbols of manhood more than a brawny squadrista who was attracted to young boys. Even if they were not homosexual, effeminate men were more despised and ridiculed because they represented the opposite of the new Fascist man who had to be self-assured, strong and tough. Largely, Fascism did not punish homosexuals but rather men who had feminine ways, and in this way it adhered without reserve to the representation of women as inferior to men. In fact, active pederasts and manly homosexuals were tolerated or at least were not persecuted, while passive pederasts were targets of repressive actions because they played the female role. Political policy viewed homosexuals as a mere secondary threat, because they limited population growth. Much more serious was the problem generated by those who, regardless of their sexual identity, spread a negative image through their womanly behaviour, thereby jeopardizing the model of respectability and manhood that Fascism projected.

SHAME REVISITED IN THE MEMORY POLITICS OF ILLIBERAL STATES

Andrea Pető

1. Jill Locke, *Democracy and the Death of Shame: Political Equality and Social Disturbance* (Cambridge, MA: Cambridge University Press, 2016), p. 171.

2. Ibid., p. 168.

3. I am aware of the fact that sexual violence was also present in the Holocaust and in the Gulag; that was the starting point of this text.

'Unashamed citizens' have been a major force behind progressive movements and revolutions. By ignoring and challenging the economy of emotions, different social groups have successfully challenged value systems that were previously seen as unchangeable. 'Unashamed citizens are not simply trying to overcome their own shame and live in a perfect, ideal state where no one ever has a bad feeling or negative emotion about themselves.'[1] 'This fantasy is tied to a highly individualistic account of moral agency as a lever for changing collective social dynamics.'[2] This social dynamics however is not static, not individualistic, and can change collective social dynamics towards exclusionary practices, not only to inclusionary practices. What is 'cool' can shift and alter from context to context. In this article I will analyze how illiberal memory politics uses the concept of shame in creating new political citizenship, by mapping how shame is narrated in relation to three traumatic events of the twentieth century: the Holocaust, the Gulag and sexual violence during the Second World War.[3] I will explore how shame is transformed in the new memory politics of illiberal states as a positive affect and how it is used as mobilization force.

The Second World War and Shame: A Changing Dynamics

I have been working on the history of sexual violence during the Second World War since the late 1990s.[4] When I started to put together a 'citation list' for a university report, I was astonished to see that an article I wrote on rapes committed by the Red Army in Hungary around 1944–1945 was my most cited article by far (both the original Hungarian, as well as its translations in German and English).[5] It was especially stunning that most of the quotes of this article on 'sexual violence' were in journals of history, and not of gender studies. With this feminist memory work, un-silencing a particular case of sexual violence faced by Hungarian women during the Second World War, I had become one of the most quoted historians by conservative and right wing academics and journalists, especially during the month of February, which marks Budapest's liberation in 1945, and the month of April, when the war in Hungary ended in 1945.

In post-1989 East Europe, there is a diverse 'market' (academic and political) for stories of brutality by the Red Army. The increasing circulation of stories of women who saw or heard other women being raped have contributed to the formation of national martyrdom. However, some of the women who had experienced sexual violence, such as Jewish women who were greeting the Red Army as liberators but were also raped, continued to remain in silence sometimes in order to not participate in the invalidation of the Red Army's role in the ending of the war. Silence for them was a form of resistance to the existing dominant politics of memory which uncritically glorified the Red Army. Their story also underlines that sometimes there are uneasy coalitions behind new memory work.[6] This new type of memory work was initiated by the illiberal turn.

To my surprise, in 2012 I was invited by a well-known pro-government journalist, Fruzsina Skrabski, to give an interview for the film she was making about the rapes committed by Red Army soldiers. The title of her project, and later the title of her film was 'Silenced Shame'.

4. Andrea Pető, *Das Unsagbäre erzählen: Sexuälle Gewalt im Ungarn in der Zweiten Weltkrieg* (Göttingen: Wallstein Verlag, forthcoming 2021).

5. Andrea Pető, 'Memory and the Narrative of Rape in Budapest and Vienna', in *Life after Death: Approaches to a Cultural and Social History of Europe during the 1940s and 1950s*, ed. Dirk Schumann and Richard Bessel (Cambridge, MA: Cambridge University Press, 2003), pp. 129–149.

6. See more Ayse Gül Altinay and Pető Andrea, 'Uncomfortable Connections: Gender, Memory, War', in *Gendered Wars, Gendered Memories: Feminist Conversations on War, Genocide and Political Violence*, ed. Ayşe Gül Altınay and Andrea Pető (New York: Routledge, 2016), pp. 1–23.

7. James M. Jasper, *The Emotions of Protest* (Chicago, IL: University of Chicago Press, 2018), p. 136.

8. Andrea Pető, 'The Lost and Found Library (Hungary)', *Mémoires en jeu⁄Memory at Stake* 9 (Summer-Fall 2019), pp. 77–82.

I immediately protested against this title: whose shame are we talking about? The women's shame, the perpetrators' shame, the relatives' shame, the collective's shame? And who silenced it? No matter that it is a judgment against the self, shame is not only an individualistic category. It is a feeling that one is perceived as inadequate or unlovable from the imagined viewpoint of the imagined others. The phrase 'facing shame' exposes the relationality inherent in the concept of shame. On the one hand, it implies confronting reality or a dimension about one's life or history that requires a change in the level of awareness about an already present reality. On the other hand, it also implies that shame is more easily recognized and encountered for what it is when a 'face' can be put on it. 'Guilt is about what I have done, shame about who I am'—as defined by Jasper.[7]

I was very much concerned about how the title of the film would contribute to the discourse about sexual violence committed by Red Army soldiers in Hungary. Apart from my article in a historical journal not much was published about these events. The mass sexual violence committed by Red Army soldiers was tabooized as soon as the war ended. From 1945 onwards, the Hungarian Communist Party commenced its ideological battle and has spoken neither about the Red Army's sexual violence nor about the Gulag. According to the then produced public myths the Soviet army brought along nothing but peace, i.e. they never engaged in violent acts against civilians.

Presently, the 'facing' of shame felt over the sexual violence committed by Red Army soldiers and the Gulag-experiences are supported by the FIDESZ government's ideology. However, the fight against shame can easily become a form of blaming. The new government-supported discourse explicitly blames 'the Russians'—representing the Red Army—for the crimes 'they' committed. In doing so they ethnicize the rape supporting Hungarian victimhood in the Second World War.

The 'facing' of shame related to the Shoah is more complicated, as the compliance of the Hungarian party with the Shoah is still debated and sometimes downright neutralized, as demonstrated by the controversial monument to the victims of the German Occupation.[8]

Before 1989, the official Hungarian history only

acknowledged victims of fascism and Nazism, i.e. Jewish victims were not acknowledged separately; only Jewish communities held separate religious commemorations. So while the Holocaust survivors are now widely seen as heroic individuals, or at least people deserving of sympathy and understanding, this was not always the case—and as I argued somewhere else it will not remain the case forever.[9] The Holocaust narrative was conceived during the Cold War, which, besides determining its characteristics, also elevated the moral command of 'Never Again' into a measure of universal integrity. The memory politics of the European Union is built on a positive notion, namely: that learning from the past is a process through which a negative experience may become a positive force. After 1989, this already canonized narrative and memory structure were exported to Eastern European countries where the actual extermination camps used to be and where the Holocaust by bullets took place. Within the framework of 'Never Again', European citizens should comply with democratic values and reject everything that led to the Holocaust. Though these values are foundational for the EU and the universal human rights paradigm, it is mostly a question of changing power dynamics whether this European memory politics can be further sustained.

　　During the 1990s, before the 2004 European Union expansion, the new member states, including the Visegrád Four countries and the Baltic States, had successfully lobbied for the acceptance of the Memorial Day for the Victims of Communism. This Memorial Day, which was expected to counterbalance the Holocaust Memorial Day, created a built-in fracture in the memory culture of Europe because particularism was inserted in a system originally based on universalism. Furthermore, as I will analyze below, this fracture indirectly contributed to rendering the collaboration of Eastern European national elites with Nazi Germany and the Soviet Union invisible. Tellingly, in Hungary both memorial days were accepted in 2000, under the first FIDESZ government.

　　The theoretical frame of different Eastern European national memory strategies, which are founded on national victimhood, varies. Countries that were occupied by both Nazi Germany and the Soviet Union

9. More on this: Andrea Pető, '"Non-Remembering" the Holocaust in Hungary and Poland', in *Poland and Hungary Jewish Realities Compared*, ed. Francois Guesnet, Howard Lupovitch, and Antony Polonsky, *Polin: Studies in Polish Jewry* 31 (2018), pp. 471–480.

REPRESSIVE ERASURE

10. Paul Connerton, 'Seven Types of Forgetting', *Memory Studies* 1, no. 1 (2008), pp. 59–71.

11. www.youtube.com/watch?v=oZTvTvGwY_4.

12. I am using 'Gulag' as an umbrella term for forced laborers collected in Hungary after 1945 by the Red Army.

13. Andrea Pető, 'Revisionist Histories: "Future Memories": Far-Right Memorialization Practices in Hungary', *European Politics and Society* 18, no. 1 (2017), pp. 41–51, doi.org/10.1080/23745118.2016.1269442

blame these two countries for all the traumas of the twentieth century. Connerton calls this process a 'repressive erasure'—a memory frame based on the exclusion of unpleasant elements of the past.[10] The Hungarian state's current memory discourse is built on this 'double occupation' framework, which is double victimization. According to this discourse, Hungary was occupied both by the Germans and the Soviets—as represented by the monument to the victims of the German occupation in Budapest on Liberty (Szabadság) Square, which was erected during the night because of public protests. The plaque, which equalizes the victims regardless whether they were Jews or Hungarian perpetrators, prompted a counter monument. The monument to the victims of the German occupation was erected in 2014 as a clear sign that the government had started a new phase in memory politics.

The film *Silenced Shame* also gained relevance in the framework of the memory politics of the Hungarian illiberal regime as it presented Hungarian women as victims of the Soviet occupation, because this turned out to be the most successful intervention in memory politics. By now every secondary school in Hungary has received a free DVD copy and Hungarian public television has broadcasted it several times. On YouTube the film has some hundred thousand views.[11]

In this paper, through three case studies—the Holocaust, the rapes committed by Red Army soldiers and the testimonies of Gulag survivors[12]—I will examine how shame is used by illiberal states. I will argue that there has been a shift in the dynamics of remembrance of illiberal memory politics: the redefinition of shame as a part of emotional politics.

New Context: The Return of (Selected) Victims

After 1989, along with the revision of progressive political traditions, anti-communism, fuelled by the memory of the persecutions that took place during the Soviet occupation, became the foundation of the emerging political discourses within the former Eastern Bloc countries.[13] Meanwhile, the various states have concealed how deeply they were historically involved in the Nazi and the communist system in order to prove that they were merely victims.

The changing frameworks of memory politics is causing theoretical and methodological difficulties in studying rapes committed during the Second World War. Using a metaphor borrowed from the natural sciences, Charles Maier discussed the 'cold' and the 'hot' memory of Nazism and communism.[14] Until 1989, the memory of Nazism was the 'hot' memory in Hungary. In other words, it was the most important framework of historiography, constructed and sustained by institutionalized memory politics (nationwide commemorations on the day of the country's liberation, wreath-laying at Soviet monuments and tombs of soldiers, etc.) Later the changing frameworks of memory politics placed other experiences and events in the centerfield of remembrance. After 1989, the emergence of museums, movies, and commemorations reminiscing the terrors of communism started to suggest that the history of communism had priority; that it had become the past that has yet be talked about. Simultaneously, the memory of Nazism became a 'cold' memory, or the memory that belonged to the past, that allegedly had no effect on the present.[15] Therefore, while the rapes committed by Soviet soldiers were a taboo topic until 1989, after 1989 they became an issue to be examined—or part of the 'hot' memory. The Gulag and the rapes committed by Red Army soldiers were missing from official history and collective memory before 1989, but they were a part of private and family histories as long as the Red Army was stationed in Hungary, until 1991. It was the burden of survivors to narrate, preserve, and transmit stories of the event: 'Oral testimony and the oral history project is the modern form of preserved communication.'[16] These stories were finally narrated after 1989—but the way they were narrated has been linked to the emergence of the 'unashamed citizen'.

Since the recent Eastern paradigm shift in Hungarian foreign politics, Russia again plays a key role as an ally. Therefore, these events are again not memorialized and possibly not talked about. (For example, *Silenced Shame* was not screened at the event organized by Angelina Jolie in London to draw attention to the victims of war time sexual violence, because the Hungarian government

14. Charles S. Maier, 'Hot Memory, Cold Memory: On the Political Half-Life of Fascist and Communist Memory', *IWM Newsletter, Transit Online* 22 (2002), www.iwm.at/transit/transit-online/hot-memory-cold-memory-on-the-political-half-life-of-fascist-and-communist-memory/.

15. More on this see Pető, 'Revisionist Histories'; Andrea Pető, 'Roots of Illiberal Memory Politics: Remembering Women in the 1956 Hungarian Revolution', *Baltic Worlds* 10, no. 4 (December 2017), pp. 42–58.

16. Michael Nutkiewicz, 'Shame, Guilt, and Anguish in Holocaust Survivor', *The Oral History Review* 30, no. 1 (Winter-Spring 2003), pp. 1–22 (p. 16).

17. Jan Assmann, 'Communicative and Cultural Memory', in *Cultural Memory Studies: An International and Interdisciplinary Handbook*, ed. Astrid Erll en Ansgar Nünning (Berlin and New York: De Gruyter, 2008), pp. 109–118.

withdrew their support for screening.) The difficulties are connected to the phenomenon that Jan Vansina calls a *floating gap*: '… there is a gap between the informal generational memory referring to the recent past and the formal cultural memory which refers to the remote past … and since this gap shifts with the succession of generations, Vansina calls it the "floating gap" … [It] illustrates the difference between social and cultural frames of memory or communicative and cultural memory.'[17] All this well exemplifies the problems that emerge when something is part of collective memory but the sources which could serve as the basis for traditional historical analysis are missing. In these cases, novels, movies, memoires, documentaries and in smaller part pictures commenced to create and recreate over and over again the memory of historical facts in an ever-changing framework, pushing what used to be 'hot' memory towards 'cold'.

The Hungarian government, together with other countries that were under German and Soviet occupation, canonized the narrative of 'double occupation', thus relegating all responsibility to the occupying forces. However, memory has multiple levels, and the local, regional, national, and transnational memories together create a multi-coloured patchwork. It is not easy to place the dark patches of the past into the ethnocentric memory politics, especially when there are competing remembrances. There is no narrative that could harmonize national historiography and the memories of the various groups of survivors. Thus, political debates turn into debates about the past; in other words: instead of talking about their party's programmes, politicians debate various interpretations of history. This of course suits the interests of the illiberal state, because in the meantime it can dynamically develop its new system of institutions. The paradigm of 'double occupation' equates the trauma of the Soviet occupation with that of the German occupation. However, all this is embedded in political processes, therefore some memories stand a better chance of becoming more dominant than others. Not all shames are equal.

Andrea Pető

Embarrassment Replacing Shame

Literature agrees that these traumas were indescribable
and unspeakable. The witnesses of the atrocities faced
many difficulties while formulating stories about what had
happened, because they were emotionally injured, unable to
adequately convey their experiences with words, or lacked
a viable frame for making their experience intelligible to
others. Yet immediately after the war, evidence shows there
were many potential storytellers but few audiences; as these
stories were undiscussable.

On the private level it was also not easy, because
survivors were also frequently silenced by strangers,
neighbours, and even family members who deemed their
experiences undiscussable as in the case of the monuments
for female victims of the Second World War in Csongrád.
The effects of these two dynamics were strikingly similar:
they transformed the survivors into a shamed group rather
than one deserving sympathy and understanding.

However, there is a difference between shame
and shame. Shame in the case of the Holocaust survivors
remains an interiorized destructive force. It is very indica-
tive that the Visual History Archive VHA is using the term
embarrassment, replacing shame.

In the case of survivors of sexual violence during
the Second World War and the stories about it or the Gulag
stories, shame is very clearly showing the face of those
who are responsible. The Soviets. Only. The stories that are
told are always the stories that happened to others. Even
if the survivors themselves gave interviews. In short: in
the case of sexual violence and Gulag the shameful stories
always happened to somebody else, and the narrators 'only'
witnessed it. In case of the Holocaust the survivors told
their own stories in a coded language. The biggest collection
of Holocaust testimonies, the Visual History Archive
does NOT use the index term shame, only embarrassment
defined as:

> A feeling of awkwardness and discomfort in one's
> acts and their imagined consequences. From the
> perspective of neuroscience, embarrassment is a
> self-conscious emotion, evoked during negative

18. See the story here: Andrea Pető, 'Digital Instruction', in Teaching about Rape in War and Genocide, ed. Carol Rittner and John K. Roth (London: Palgrave, 2016), pp. 91–93.

19. See more Pertti Ahonen, et al., *People on the Move: Forced Population Movements in Europe in the Second World War and its Aftermath* (Oxford and New York: Berg Publisher, 2008).

evaluation following norm violations and social transgressions and recruits brain regions representing social conceptual knowledge.

Although shame was mentioned several times by the interviewees, it remained invisible in the indexing. Exactly the same happened with the concept of rape.[18] When I used the VHA for my course on gendering the Holocaust, my students searched for the index term 'rape' but they only found 'sexual assault'. After I sent my students' final papers—of course with their permission—to the VHA, it took them another four years to re-index the stories as rape. Re-indexing revised the concept and definition of rape. This story leads us to the question of invisibilization by indexing.

From the 52,000 interviews accessible online there were less than sixty testimonies that mentioned or were labelled as 'embarrassment'. Some of these stories in which shame was explicitly mentioned made the indexer decide to label them with the term 'embarrassment', even though the term was not explicitly mentioned in them. Interestingly, the explicit mentioning of the feeling of shame was more common *after* the liberation than before. Before, the stories were connected to exposing naked bodies, or being harassed on the street by anti-Semitic mobs.

The occupying Red Army forcibly deported 600,000 Hungarians to make up for the loss in its labour force.[19] The fate of these civilians, and that of the Hungarian POWs, was the subject of one of the major public debates after 1945 until the communist takeover. Then the fate and the return of the Hungarian workers was tabooized. Those who returned received any financial compensation or political rehabilitation only after the collapse of communism. Therefore, the collection of documents and testimonies started very late after the events. Today, when Putin's Russia is whitewashing the crimes committed by the Soviet Regime, this research and memorialization process are getting more and more difficult. It is one of the reasons that the survivors' stories are not collected and very few are available for research. I also looked at the Gulag stories accessible online, which are considerably less in number, and shame has not been mentioned at all as that would perpetuate

INTERGENERATIONAL TRAUMA

the victory of the Soviets. One story mentioned shame explicitly: a deeply religious man who used his Bible's pages to make cigarettes, which he exchanged for food.

Conclusions

What are the similarities of the testimonies about these three traumatic events? How does shame manifest in these three cases and what are the consequences if the 'unashamed citizens' are silencing those who should have been speaking about the events?

In the past years, political scientists and analysts scrutinizing the impressive series of electoral victories of illiberal powers globally were forced to reconsider their conceptual tools when trying to understand the new phenomenon of 'democratic authoritarianism', 'hybrid regime', 'illiberal state', or 'mafia state'. Together with the Polish sociologist Weronika Grzebalska we compared Hungary and Poland, and based on our findings we argued that we are facing a new form of governance, which stems from the failures of globalized (neo)liberal democracy including its politics of emotions.[20] Based on its modus operandi, we called this regime an 'illiberal polypore state', because as a parasite, it feeds on the vital resources of the previous political system and at the same time actively contributes to its decay by setting up parallel institutions and redirecting resources into them. So here is nothing new here. The polypore state, by controlling hegemonic forms of remembrance, works within the framework of what is referred to as 'mnemonic security'.[21] The translation of history and its application and thus their identity-shaping effect, are becoming a geopolitical factor. This is especially true about the memory of the Second World War and the Holocaust: polypore states set up lavishly funded historical films, new historical research institutes, and museums that have no professional quality assurance; and decreased the state funding of pre-existent internationally recognized institutions. Memory politics plays a key role in this process. Different states are silencing stories about their own techniques of discrimination that were inherent parts of their history in order to prove that they were victims.

20. Weronika Grzebalska and Andrea Pető, 'The Gendered Modus Operandi of the Illiberal Transformation in Hungary and Poland', *Women's Studies International Forum* 68 (May-June 2018), pp. 164–172, doi.org/10.1016/j.wsif.2017.12.001.

21. Maria Mälksoo, '"Memory Must Be Defended": Beyond the Politics of Mnemonical Security', *Security Dialogue* 46, no. 3 (2015), pp. 221–237.

The memory politics of the 'polypore state' is to duplicate, depoliticize, and empty the narrative and historical agency by appropriating its meanings. In this historical context it attributes new meanings of victimhood and anti-communism. It also takes over and empties the concept of shame. This illiberal memory politics functions within the framework of new emotional economies, where the concept of shame plays a new role.

The sooner we recognize that there has been an intervention in and by shame culture, the earlier the change may happen. The floating gap should float with active intervention of feminist scholars and activists as 'unashamed citizens'. If we stick to Vansina's metaphor, the floating gap always includes different experiences and is always floating towards something else. That at least is a hopeful sign for the future.

An earlier version of this text was presented at the conference: 'Shame—Shaming—Shamelessness: International Conference by the Research Network "Gender and Agency"', at University of Vienna, 30 November 2019.

Monument to the victims of the German occupation, Szabadság Square, Budapest

MARLENE
DUMAS

Only Good Friends, 1990
mixed media on paper, 18 x 29 cm

Apology, 2001
ink and ink wash on paper, 21 x 15.5 cm

Things Men Do, 2001
ink wash and acrylic on paper, 45 x 35 cm

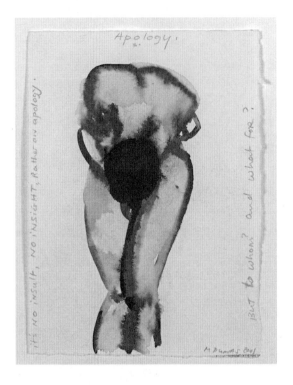

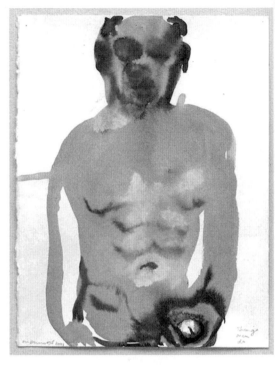

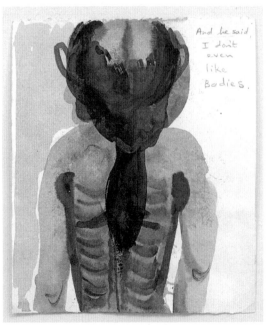

And He Said I Don't Even Like Bodies, 1994
ink and acrylic on paper, 28 x 24.5 cm

The Hairy Phallus, 1989
ink, crayon and pencil on paper, 31.9 x 24 cm

The Sexuality of Christ, 1994
ink and acrylic on paper, 28 x 24.5 cm

Marlene Dumas

'en mijn liefdes zijn
louter taal van zinnen, gekneld
tussen sacrale plooien van lust,
sadistisch, masochistisch
De broeken met hun lauwe zak
waarin het lot van een man
getekend list —   '
                                    — Pasolini

Pasolini, 1988
ecoline on paper, 29.5 x 21 cm

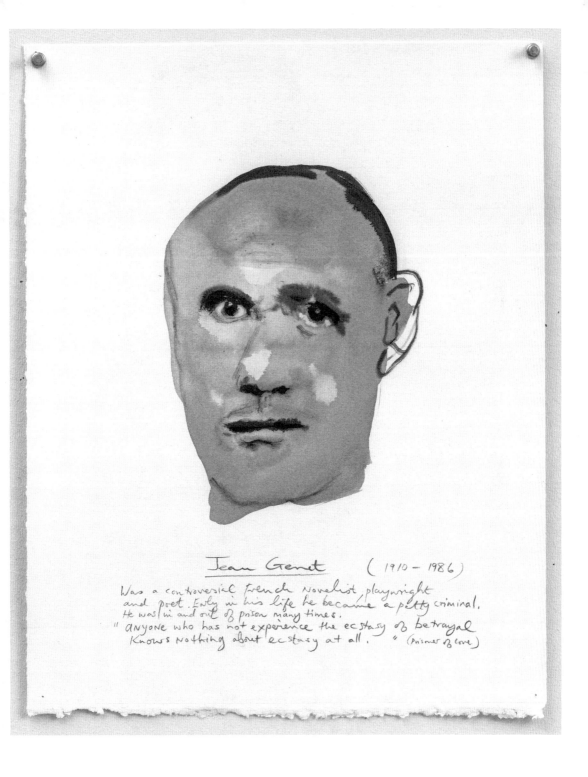

Jean Genet   (1910 - 1986)

Was a controversial French novelist playwright
and poet. Early in his life he became a petty criminal.
He was in and out of prison many times.
" anyone who has not experience the ecstasy of betrayal
knows nothing about ecstasy at all. " (Prisoner of love)

Marlene Dumas

Jean Genet (from the series *Great Men*), 2014
ink, metallic acrylic and pencil on paper,
44 x 35 cm

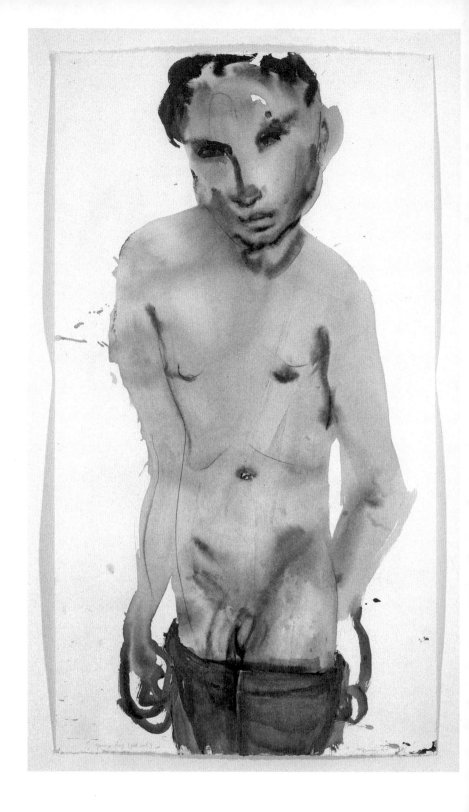

SHAME! and Masculinity

Young Boy (Wet Suit), 1996
ink and ink wash on paper, 125 x 70 cm

He burns with bashful shame, she with her tears
Doth quench the maiden burning of his cheeks;
Then with her windy sighs and golden hairs
To fan and blow them dry again she seeks.
      He saith she is immodest, blames her miss;
      What follows more, she murders with a kiss.

excerpt from
William Shakespeare's *Venus and Adonis*

Adonis blushes, 2015–2016
ink wash and metallic acrylic
on paper, 29.5 x 22 cm

This is one of the illustra-
tions that Marlene Dumas
made especially for the
Dutch translation by Hafid
Bouazza of *Venus and
Adonis* (Athenaeum, 2016).

FATHER SHAME?
In Search of Post-Patriarchal Authority

Maaike Meijer

A surprising number of Dutch/Flemish contemporary
male thinkers about the dynamic of gender relations are
well-versed in psychoanalysis: Paul Verhaeghe and Frank
Koerselman are psychiatrists, and Bart Vieveen is a cultural
studies scholar leaning on Lacanian psychoanalysis.
Sociologist Abram de Swaan has worked as a psychoanalyst
and frequently brings psychoanalytic ideas into his work.
In addition, three out of these four have a feminist outlook.
Since psychoanalysis has long been an instrument of
inequality between genders, the question arises if and how
these authors manage to make the psychoanalytic toolkit
useable for a critical view of the relations between the sexes.
Moreover, they agree that we live in, or are on our way to
a 'post-patriarchy'. What future do they imagine? Will the
world be a better place where people can be equal as well as
different, where no one needs to be ashamed of what they
are? Will men still be ashamed for being small or physically
vulnerable? Because they cry or show fear? Because they
cannot keep a close-enough watch on their sisters or
spouses? Will women still be ashamed because they have
been unable to net a guy, because they cannot match the
current ideal of beauty, because the people around them
condemn their independence?

The answers depend on whom you ask. According
to Koerselman our society is de-fathering itself: paternal
values such as belief in hierarchy and perseverance are
no longer transmitted, and for him that is a problem.
These days, fathers must adapt to a new 'feminine' norm

of indulgence and egalitarianism. They dare no longer be fathers. They suffer from 'father shame'. Koerselman calls for a revaluation of traditional fatherhood. In his view it is not the old patriarchal society that produces shame, but on the contrary, for him it is the feminized post-patriarchal world that does so.

De-Fathering and the Creation of Shame

Koerselman tells the following childhood memory in an interview on the occasion of his short book *Ontvadering* (De-fathering):

> A boy at our school had committed suicide and social helpers came to talk with the students about the shock this had caused. In the sixties. 'So, that was already done back then', says Frank Koerselman. He was himself also pretty hard hit by the event, and when it kept him awake at night his mother sent him to the GP. 'A bully', says Koerselman. 'You know what he said?' He leans forwards in his chair. 'Are we going to BE A SISSY?' He laughs and leans back again. 'That GP', he says, 'was totally right. And my problem was immediately gone.'

Hence, hurray for the bully. For me, that GP *creates* shame. A boy who is shocked by the suicide of a classmate is going to be a sissy, so he is going to repress that response. That creates the so-called real boys, who are ashamed of their emotions.

A more empathic reaction would have been appropriate. Why was the young Koerselman so affected? Perhaps this was his first confrontation with death; perhaps another shock, guilt, or need was underlying it. After the rhetorical question, 'are we going to be a sissy?' he will never find out. Another doctor could have helped him to express his feelings and thereby release himself from a suffocating emotional constriction. The message 'your life continues' can be part of that. By the way, assisting a child is not reducible to fatherliness. Here, not so much gender but age

1. Jannetje Koelewijn, 'Een vader moet flink zijn.' [A father should be tough: Interview with Frank Koerselman], *NRC Handelsblad*, 26 February 2020.

and professionalism are involved. A woman GP could have done the same thing, either bully or show empathy. But Koerselman turns this encounter into a lesson in patriarchy between a fatherly authority and his boy pupil.

I suppose Koerselman sees me now as a representative of that overly maternal world, which has called for the reaction allowing the Trumps to grab their chance.

> '[Trump,] the absolute example of the narcissistic, immature father who came to power thanks to the "horizontal, inclusive, identitarian leftist movement". That is not an incident. Where in the world do we still see mature and wise fathers as leaders? Wherever I turn, I don't see them.'
>
> **[Interviewer:]** 'Angela Merkel?'
>
> 'Merkel?' Koerselman spreads his arms. 'Just come in, *wir schaffen das*. Isn't that a mother? That is *the* mother. And she didn't manage it. If she had, things would have been different. But she didn't manage it.'[1]

But was the '*wir schaffen das*' a 'motherly', indulgent message? To whom was that statement directed? If she is speaking to refugees, one can imagine that Merkel reassures them: 'Come on in, we will manage to host you. You don't have to do anything for that.' But to me, the message seems directed, rather, to Merkel's fellow Germans: we can do this! In other words, be tough, don't whine, do it. We can show what we are worth. Extraordinarily 'paternal' if you wish to think in those terms, but especially just clear and brave. This is a leader speaking. But if it comes from women, Koerselman finds it by definition soft and egalitarian. In addition, he settles accounts with Merkel about the resistance her successful integration project ended up soliciting. As if she was responsible for that resistance. According to such reasoning you can also call Nelson Mandela a failed leader. No, Koerselman does not belong to the feminists in this group. I will return to his 2019 book *Ontvadering* below.

Groundless Patriarchal Authority

> We barely realize it, but we are living at the end
> of an era. We say goodbye to the patriarchal form
> of authority that for roughly ten thousand years
> has determined everything, sexually, socially, reli-
> giously, politically, economically. This doesn't mean
> that we say goodbye to authority. For [Hannah]
> Arendt no society can do without authority,
> because its function is to regulate the relations
> among people. (p. 61)

Quoted here is Paul Verhaeghe, professor of clinical
psychology and psychoanalysis, from his 2015 book
Autoriteit (Authority), which was reprinted many times.
He offers an encompassing analysis of the erosion of
patriarchy in Western society, which for him is an irreversible process. Authority can only function if the majority
believes in it. For the traditional masculine form of vertical
authority that majority doesn't exist anymore. The old
power strongholds and Christian values have melted into
air due to the neoliberal values of money and success. At
the same time, the inequality between men and women
has gradually diminished. This has brought women more
financial self-determination, hence, more divorce and fewer
traditional families, more higher-educated girls, more boys
with learning disabilities and behavioural disorders, more
single mothers who prefer to do it alone or together than
with a recalcitrant man, more singles. The privileges and
power of men, once so self-evident, are being contested. But
at the same time, our society has a problem of authority,
according to Verhaeghe. People don't listen anymore to the
old authorities: fathers, priests, teachers, doctors, and police
officers; yet, a society cannot be without forms of accepted
authority. How do we solve that problem?
    The answer cannot be 'get rid of father shame'
or 'back to the zero of patriarchy', although the call for
restauration of the old values is loud and clear. Dutch
political movements such as those of Fortuyn, Wilders and
Baudet all want to return to patriarchal gender relations.
Abram de Swaan, sociologist and former psychoanalyst,
considers this a worldwide backlash against the rise of

women, in his 2019 book *Tegen de vrouwen* (Against women). Men feel hurt, humiliated, and dishonoured. De Swaan pays much attention to the collective psychological consequences of women's emancipation for men. They strike back with extreme-right political movements, restoration of misogynist religions, group rape, confinement and other forms of curtailment of women. But, De Swaan predicts, the emancipation of women is unstoppable all over the world. For him this is the beginning of a better world. Verhaeghe agrees, but limits himself to the Western world. He is not so much focused on the fierce resistance of men, but reflects on the new post-patriarchal forms of authority that society needs.

First, Verhaeghe wants to know where, in fact, that vanished paternal authority came from. He does not look at the division of tasks determined by evolution, but at the power of law and habit. Men have been boss for a very long time. Why? Because! Patriarchal power has no ground to stand on, and whoever searches for that ground discovers that it doesn't exist. Paternal power is paradoxically grounded in patricide. Verhaeghe derives that from Freud, who in *Totem and Taboo* from 1912 'places the origin of authority in the originary act of violence against the father' (p. 42). There was a 'primal father' who not only kept the women for himself but also oppressed the sons. The brotherhood killed the tyrannical father and declared a new law that restricted the inter-male violence and thus facilitated living together. Afterwards, out of guilt, they idealized the father, deified him—which is, according to Freud, the origin of monotheistic religions. The omnipotent father is thus a retrospective construction, a fantasy, designed by the guilty sons. They instituted the law, and placed the source of authority with a higher unquestionable authority: God.

> It's striking: in the original version, half of the ten commandments oblige the believers to obedience to the divine father, in combination with an absolute and exclusive loyalty. ... The argument is circular: God is the source of authority because He commands us to obey Him and only Him. (p. 44)

The reasoning in the Code of Hammurabi, the oldest known legislation, is just as circular. There, it says that the supreme gods

> have appointed the king 'to make justice triumph in the land ... and to prevent the strong from oppressing the weak.' The king and his ... laws have the force of law because the supreme deities wish it that way—*says the king.* (p. 46)

In his analysis of the source of patriarchal authority Verhaeghe demonstrates the surplus value of his psychoanalytic perspective. Bookcases have been filled with writings about Freud's *Totem and Taboo*, but still, the idea that the establishment of paternal authority was a retrospective construction and a power grab that could only work as long as people believe in it, seems a plausible one. After that, male authority can only be maintained by the use of violence (see De Swaan). Authority that rests on a shared set of convictions does not need violent means to maintain itself. In this, Verhaeghe follows Hannah Arendt. According to Verhaeghe, the beginning of contestation of patriarchal authority began with the Enlightenment, with Kant's appeal to every individual to think for themselves. The resistance movements of the 1960s are just an exclamation mark added to a much longer process that led to women's emancipation and democracy, but in our time also to demanding school students who don't want to obey anyone any longer, to citizens screaming at the police, to a crisis in education where teachers have it increasingly hard, where school and parents argue about who should exercise authority. There is a crisis of authority. A void of authority.

Deploring De-Fathering

This view echoes the state of things sketched by Verhaeghe's fellow psychiatrist Koerselman. The latter, however, advocates the restoration of paternal authority, as opposed to Verhaeghe and De Swaan. He invokes Alexander Mitscherlich's book from 1963, *Society without the Father.* Mitscherlich—again a psychoanalyst—has seen the dethroning of the fathers coming, long before 'May '68'. For him the cause of the problem of the absent fathers was the decline of the traditional society of farmers and craftsmen. There, labour and home duties still converged; there, sons could succeed their fathers, like the craftsmen their masters. But the industrial revolution took the father away from the home front. 'That, as it were, broke the hierarchical spine of the family', as Koerselman paraphrases Mitscherlich. If, on top of it all, women start to work, all bindings evaporate and all that's left is sibling rivalry, without any authority structure. While in 1963 Mitscherlich saw the disappearance of fatherly authority coming, according to Koerselman, since then an entire generation of children without control have grown into irresolute adults, living in a horizontal society of equality. Koerselman is mostly talking about wavering sons who don't know any limits anymore. Therefore, they cannot defend themselves against competition and setbacks, which for Koerselman explains the burnout epidemic. Everyone calls everyone by first names, children are pampered to the extreme. Contemporary leaders don't endorse their own authority. Police officers and professional rescue workers cannot do their jobs anymore, because other 'equals' do not obey their orders. Horizontality, according to Koerselman, is a 'feminine' principle, whereas verticality is allegedly 'masculine'. To be fair, Koerselman writes that the traditional masculine repertoire does not have to be fulfilled by men at all costs; as long as at least someone fills the void.

That point could make Koerselman an interesting interlocutor, but alas: for him, authority remains bound to masculinity. He impedes himself by erecting a mythical, pinkish image of the nuclear family, where the mother provides warmth and care, the father keeps the family safe, and leads the child into the world with his orders and interdictions. His image is completely dualistic. Mother inside, father outside in the environment. At first, Koerselman follows Mitscherlich, who saw industrialization as a breach with this idyll. But then he comes up with a different story of origin: patriarchy emerged in the prehistoric steppe, where mother breastfed and cared, while father deployed physical force; that is the 'primal family'. That projection of the modern nuclear family onto prehistory—where, as is well known, people did not live in families but in groups—serves to build up that pink myth, as does the thesis that fathers guide children to the outside by

> [t]he transmission of knowledge and the skills of the crafts. That comes with challenging and holding back, with criticism and praise, with solidarity and competition. The father teaches his child to be responsible in the sense of courageous and wise, militant and controlled. In that primal family, the father also acquaints the child with norms and values. Where mother forgives, father is the one who punishes. Where mother loves all children equally, father practices a hierarchy of merit. Mother's love knows no law; father's love is the law. In this way, both satisfy fundamental needs. (p. 26)

As happens more often, knowledge, skills, and crafts are here unquestionably attributed to men, whereas women have always had an enormous share in technologies such as agriculture, making fire and food, finding medicines, creating body warmth. It is a gross distortion to attribute the entire domain of knowledge and craft wholesale to 'father'. That is itself the result of the historic expulsion of women from science and technology, in an attempt to inflect these into exclusively masculine areas. Koerselman shares this tendency blindly. It is just as wrong to imagine that mothers would not impose rules on their children, would not punish them, not teach them to deal with danger, to develop skills and crafts, nor transmit norms and values to them. All that belongs to that kitschy-pink story that floats on a mythical difference between the sexes. Above all, it is totally ahistorical.

Koerselman's image of fathers and mothers coincides entirely with the nineteenth-century Western bourgeois ideal where the ideology of separate spheres reached its zenith. That is his point of reference. That everything has changed during the past century is a problem. Male muscle strength has become redundant and the anti-conception pill has terminated the inevitability of motherhood. Women also claimed the world outside, and yes, yes, that creates welfare and is good for women—he is willing to concede that. But, he wonders, why do horizontal and vertical worlds keep being gendered, hence, female and male domains respectively? Why don't men do more domestic work? Why do they flee feminine professions? Because... nature cannot be overruled, it seems!

In this argument there is not a trace of political awareness or commitment. Are we unable to eliminate hunger from the world? Nature must have wanted it that way. Do men continue to indulge in gang rape? Nature speaks. This psychiatrist resigns himself a priori to unequal opportunities, discrimination, unequal salaries, rock-hard glass ceilings, and, even stranger, suggests at the same time that these things don't exist anymore. Feminism has been excessively successful:

> This leads to the historically perhaps unique situation that the old-style motherly values also came to dominate public life. For the current Western society has become horizontal, inclusive, and free of traditional norms. Hierarchy, selectivity, and tradition have been pushed into the defensive everywhere. Thus, patriarchy yields to matriarchy. (p. 60)

This is clearly inconsistent: first the equality between man and women failed because nature could not be overruled, and then we are saddled with a fully-grown matriarchy nevertheless? But apart from being inconsistent, the final statement of this passage is too naive for words. We are far from having achieved gender equality. Women barely ever reach the top. The gap in payment is enormous. But no; the real problem is that 'politically-correct wave of father shame' (p. 77) that floods us. I don't believe it at all. Men who take their father role seriously are often appreciated in their own circle, but they get little understanding and little space for their parenting from those 'motherly' (?) businesses where they work.

Koerselman considers the 'de-fathering' a symptom of regression:

Where the paternal vertical domain has withered and is, so to speak, being overgrown by the horizontal domain ... the disappearance of the sexual difference is to be expected. Gender fluidity doesn't make it any easier to even recognize fathers—let alone that children can identify as boys or girls. (p. 70)

The language becomes quite suggestive here: 'overgrown' (the feminine as ineradicable weeds) and matriarchy as a terrifying image. That the binary of sexual difference can no longer be the measure of all things frightens Koerselman, and in that respect he reveals himself as a super-conservative psychoanalyst.

Alternative Forms of Shame

For me—and also for analysts such as Verhaeghe and De Swaan—relativized gender difference is rather liberating. It does not erase differences among people but, on the contrary, it gives those differences more space. De Swaan phrases it thus:

I prefer to live in a world where I can encounter people I can appreciate for their own merits, their special features, their unique personality that is complex, never entirely fathomable, never quite predictable, and internally contradictory. I prefer that to a world in which what kind of person you have before you is already determined once you know to what group they belong. I want to appreciate people for who they are, not for what they are. (p. 11)

A society kept cohesive by dogmatic gender difference thrives on shame as a disciplining emotion. Within the individual, cultural dogmas work as an Ideal-ego, an interior sentry. You are ashamed of all behaviours and emotions that fall outside of the norm. You fear rejection, exclusion from the group. A society that gives more space to individuality diminishes shame and nourishes self-esteem.

There will always be some measure of Ideal-ego in our lives—its content can slowly change, as has been happening for decades now in the West, due to oppressive images of bodily perfection and social success. On a large scale, God has been replaced by the values of neo-liberal capitalism—for which our interior has become the new colonial empire. Also, those who resist this are likewise guided by an Ideal-ego that can in turn produce shame: shame of flying, shame of consumption. The latter forms of shame seem to me less paralyzing, because they are based on a political choice. That a newly-installed feminist conscience could produce shame in men due to their being-men seems a rare phenomenon to me. It was once presented as a parody in the sketch 'Men's consciousness-raising group' by Dutch satirists Van Kooten and De Bie. It was hilarious, and the message was clear: guys, sympathize with women, but by all means, don't be ashamed! 'Father-shame', a shyness to practice fathering I have yet to encounter in anyone I know. I know proud fathers, fathers who are ill at ease, happy fathers, tired fathers, sperm donors who have grown into welcome fathers. To be sure, there are still unwilling fathers, given the many mothers who are craving the participation of their spouses in the care for their joint offspring. On average, men shirk parenting more easily than mothers, but that is not what father-shame is about. The old patriarchal fathers do not know shame. They were simply shamelessly bossy.

Koerselman deploys his psychoanalytic knowledge especially to sketch a typology of fathers, from fathers who are primary narcissists (adolescent, immature) and secondary narcissists (too domineering) who indulge in 'narcissistic rage', up to mature, stimulating fathers. His ideal is the wise father who 'dares show that toughness, self-control and self-relativizing are virtues of which you should still be proud'. That's the kind of fathers we need. Fine by me. Only, this is about *parenthood*. Mothers transmit these virtues just as much. But the initial idea, that the values that up to then were considered paternal can also be incarnated by women has by now disappeared far beyond the horizon. Koerselman's discourse drips nostalgia for the wise father. Nostalgia is a longing for something that has never really existed. The second chance he wishes to give fathers is clad in utopian expectations. This is what Freud would call a *Familienroman*, which is conjured up, precisely, by failing or absent fathers. It is the fairy-tale of the good, just father, a fantasy that is inherent in all monotheistic religions; an idealized father image, which is here confused with reality. Verhaeghe already showed us how patriarchy can have emerged from guilty sons who idealized their father and posthumously bestowed absolute power on him. It is possible and illuminating to consider Verhaeghe's book as a (psycho)analysis of Koerselman's.

AN AUTHORITY VOID?
Share the Power with Women

It seems clear that a society needs broadly-supported forms of authority. I also recognize the phenomenon of a post-patriarchal lack of authority. But in my view, authority doesn't work well now because something went wrong in the attempt to really share power with women. Men have shared their power only grudgingly, too slowly, too reluctantly, insufficiently. Women have been sabotaged in many areas. They have not been able to seize authority because they could not conquer it. Where women should have stood as fellow authorities, now stands a man who is no longer entitled to it alone. He can earn that position through merit, but too often it is given to him on the groundless basis of his being a man. This rubs many the wrong way. It's wrong. In domains where women do predominate—such as education—their authority is subject to doubt. Plus, it is considered a problem that education 'feminizes'. Health care is, similarly, a national waste pit.

That so many domains have traditionally been filled and determined by men has never been seen as a problem. Well, true, when it all went down the drain in the banking sector you could sometimes hear people say that the male hegemony was not entirely unrelated. But this insight has barely had any consequences. It should have stopped long since, this elbowing by men, but it never did. Courage, wisdom, generosity, honesty, the guts to give your fellow men a good talking-to about their reluctance—what happened to those beautiful 'masculine' features that had made a redistribution possible? That's where the problem lies.

In short, the authority void is related to the lack of serious sharing of power with women. In the West, May '68 was successful for men, but only halfway for women. There is the promise of equality, and there is a reality that belies it only too often. That is why no one knows in what kind of world he or she really lives.

All this is, of course, also a bad basis for establishing equality with people of colour, refugees, and migrants. The creation of a democratic world has been halted halfway. We must carry on with it. And in that sense, we can, again, learn a lot from Paul Verhaeghe, who sees promising post-patriarchal forms of authority emerge.

Verhaeghe considers three democratizing domains: firstly, raising children; secondly, economy and management; and thirdly, politics. His vision of education and child-rearing from the principle 'it takes a village to raise a child' is particularly catching. In this view, parenting and education are best seen, today, as teamwork. There, what matters is proximity and group connections, where the 'difficult' child is not placed outside the group, with or without psychiatric problem-naming labels, but on the contrary, is kept inside it. When children know they belong to a live connection with parents and co-parents, real or adopted grannies and granddads, stepfamilies, school mistresses, masters and neighbours who join forces to transform home and school into liveable places, a lot less would go wrong than it currently does. In this story gender only plays a part in Verhaeghe's examples of unsettled children; boys mostly, given the over-representation of boys among children who are going wrong. Verhaeghe's solution does not come from fathers but from a diverse group of parental figures. Such groups are not composed on the basis of gender, then, but on the basis of age and degree of involvement.

Just as contagious is his vision of the sustainability of the economy and the horizontal management of companies. That story is full of practical examples demonstrating that the world can turn without macho leaders, without debt explosions and addiction to growth, and that many businesses already function democratically, with more contentment among workers and more success. In the political domain, Verhaeghe's plea is for a deliberative democracy where people decide together about the world they share, according to the model of the 'commons', the pasturages around the village that our ancestors used together for their cattle. In all these domains authority can be based on horizontally organized groups, which together develop a practice or invent a regulation to which everyone submits more or less voluntarily. Then, authority is no longer masculine and vertical, but horizontal and shared among men and women, Verhaeghe predicts and advocates. Then the individual will be able to see her- or himself in bonding with others. Verhaeghe's psychological vision of safe attachment as the basis of subjectivity, of the interplay of connection and separation—deducting the over-estimation of individualism—backs this democratic image of the future.

FRATRIARCHY?
The Liberation of Psychoanalysis

De Swaan and Verhaeghe liberate psychoanalysis and give it a renewed social relevance. Koerselman makes do with a version that is long past its expiration date. A fourth Dutch post-patriarchal thinker who has recently described the vanishing of the classical father figure is Bart Vieveen. Under the title *De ontvoogding van de tragische held* (The emancipation of the tragic hero), he does not trace the abdication of the paternal authority in social domains, but in prominent cultural imaginings. He analyzes F. Bordewijk's Character from 1938, Gerard Reve's *The Evenings* from 1949, and Tom Lanoye's rewriting of Shakespeare in *Hamlet versus Hamlet naar Shakespeare* from 2014, respectively.

In Lanoye's *Hamlet* Vieveen reads a provisional endpoint of a development, namely the emergence of a new *horizontal* authority, where young men bestow on one another an identity in the symbolic order and endorse, as equals, a new ground for authority. It is in the direction of such a psychological constellation that we are currently moving. This vision of a post-patriarchal future resonates with Verhaeghe's. Vieveen addresses a specialized audience of people knowledgeable in Lacanian psychoanalysis. His heavily jargon-spiced PhD dissertation contains beautiful essays. His analysis of *Character*—the confrontation between the bailiff Dreverhaven and his bastard son Katadreuffe—is fascinating. The different versions of the book constantly change their emphasis. The original serial publication from 1928 primarily tells the story of the father, a harsh debt collector who purposely inflicts bankruptcy on his son, and challenges him to kill him. He is an old man, tired of life, who seeks a last satisfaction in the struggle with his son. But the son refuses the dagger and thereby refuses to play his part in the patriarchal succession in which sons must vanquish their fathers in order to conquer their place. Katadreuffe declines all roles in that father-son constellation, but then, who is he? Is he not himself sitting on the branch of the tree that he is sawing off? In subsequent versions—the novel from 1938, the film from 1997—the story is told from the perspective of the son. During the final confrontation he is almost murdered by his father, but at the *moment suprême*, he demonstrates deep contempt for him. This unsettles Dreverhaven. It is not the son who is dependent on the father, but the other way around. Dreverhaven commits suicide. But Katadreuffe is no longer interested in cashing in on his victory. For he has already positioned himself totally outside of the patriarchal masculine line of succession.

One thing seems odd: the dismantling of patriarchy has enormous consequences for the positions of both sons and women, who will be able to participate legitimately as equals in post-patriarchal society, which gives the world a new democratic foundation. Strangely, however, this aspect receives scant attention in Vieveen's analysis. Central, for him, is the emancipation of the sons and the disorientation this entails for them. That makes sense, of course. But Vieveen almost totally overlooks women. However nuanced the analysis of the different versions of *Character* may be, what Vieveen under-illuminates is the position of Katadreuffe's mother Joba. She is the one who had cut off her connection to Dreverhaven (who had raped her) already much earlier. She is the one who saw through him from the start, who rejected all forms of dependency, who chose the path of autonomy, and let her son stand on his own legs right away. She didn't need anything from that man. So, she is the one who immediately saw that the promises patriarchy makes to its subjects are deceptive and ugly. Katadreuffe follows in the footsteps of his mother.

In Hamlet, Vieveen sees the emergence of a society of brothers. But the way Hamlet mocks his beloved Ophelia as representative of the treacherousness of all women, and sends her away—'Get thee to a nunnery'—is not rewritten in Lanoye's constellation of Hamlet. That speech to Ophelia is one of the harshest anti-woman tirades in world literature. Hamlet projects onto Ophelia, who had no share in it whatsoever, his powerless rage about the murder of his father, committed by his uncle with the complicity of his mother. Vieveen interprets this as that Hamlet can no longer love Ophelia. Suddenly he can no longer see her with idealizing eyes. But Hamlet's gaze is something else than the sobering look of a realist fallen out of love; it is the hatred against uncle and mother that he dumps onto Ophelia. Vieveen seems blind to that classical projection on women as a group. Ophelia is a fellow sufferer and contemporary of Hamlet, but she is not allowed into the brotherhood. Patriarchy becomes a fratriarchy. That in itself is a patriarchal reflex.

Vieveen does not problematize that exclusion of women, and thus repeats the empty spot already present in Freud's *Totem and Taboo*: the 'primal father' was already a projection, as Verhaeghe explained. The masculine brothers commit patricide and proceed to venerate the father posthumously, so that 'his authority [shines] on all later fathers, who thereby can also become little primary fathers', as he remarks ironically (p. 43). In this way it looks as if the daughters and the sons liberate themselves from patriarchy, each in their own way, without developing a bond with one another as fellow sufferers.

How can we make sure patriarchy does not transform into fratriarchy? How can men shed the illusions of the male-line succession system, for good? The social process of deep democratization has barely begun. And in spite of all declarations that patriarchy is entirely or almost dismantled: we are not done with the rewriting of psychoanalysis by far.

References

Frank Koerselman, *Ontvadering: Het einde van de vaderlijke autoriteit* (Amsterdam: Prometheus. 2020)

Abram de Swaan, *Tegen de vrouwen: De wereldwijde strijd van rechtsisten en jihadisten tegen de emancipatie* (Amsterdam: Prometheus, 2019)

Paul Verhaeghe, *Autoriteit* (Amsterdam: De Bezige Bij, 2015)

Bart Vieveen, *De ontvoogding van de tragische held: Hamlet, Katadreuffe en Van Egters verkennen de grenzen van het bedreigde Vader-land* (Antwerp and Apeldoorn: Garant, 2019)

Maaike Meijer

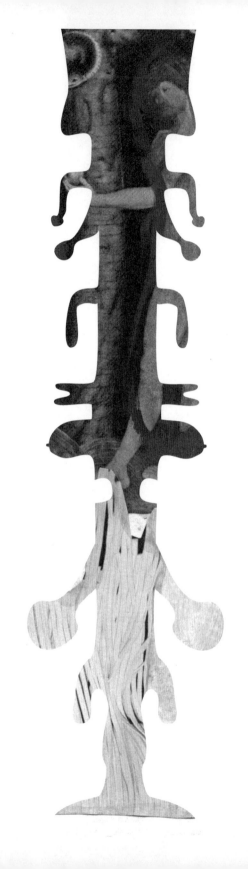

MY GRANDFATHER'S OFFICE

Adeola Enigbokan

When I knew my grandfather, he was a retired trade unionist, having come up through the heady days of Nigeria's independence from colonial rule. His major work had been to help organize cocoa farmers of the Yoruba towns and villages of western Nigeria. Cocoa was one of the Nigerian colony's cash crops, and yet the workers were some of the most undervalued in the country. The right of workers to organize unions had become law only in 1938, and the 1940s and 1950s were a turbulent, promising time as workers and trade unionists built solidarity, learned to lead themselves, and to demand better labour conditions. For my grandfather this would have meant traveling around the region and the world, meeting and learning from other workers and trade union leaders, giving lectures and workshops, organizing summer schools and public discussions and writing lots and lots of letters. By 1960, the year of Nigerian independence from Great Britain, my grandfather was secretary general of the Western Nigeria Development Corporation and Allied Industries Workers' Union.

In the 1980s, Joseph Oladipo Enigbokan was a neat, quiet man. I could never imagine him giving a public speech. His room was simple and orderly, the bed always made, a clean piece of paper and pen placed on his small writing table. The desk in his office downstairs, was much larger, but just as neat, with carefully placed paper weights, souvenirs from his travels to unite workers of the world. I was especially fascinated with his writing tools: the fountain pen which he refilled regularly, and the slim, elegant letter opener, its polished darkness resting heavily in the palm of my hand. But mostly I did not play with my grandfather's things, except the house telephone, which sat at the edge of the desk, and always tempted me to make up number games with its rotary dial. And the globe of the world, which would spin so beautifully on its wooden axis, the entire world whizzing by in pastel colours.

From some of his pictures, in a fez maybe, with a group of serious, dark-suited men in white shirts and thin ties,

I could conjure panelled conference rooms, in Moscow, Hanoi, or Addis Ababa, in the 1950s and 1960s, where non-aligned leaders of working people from around Africa and the world met to talk strategy, how to navigate together the emerging postcolonial world. The air was dense with smoke and newly found power. And the core desire of those meetings, conducted in a cacophony of languages, might have been how to restore dignity to the lives of men and women shaped by the politics and economics of colonial rule, that most shameful form of governance. A career spent in rooms like this, or alongside cocoa farmers in their fields, and on factory floors and in union halls, hearing the stories of workers, trying to improve their conditions during the crucial years of Nigeria's transition from colony to independent nation, would have shaped his body and his manner into that of the upright elderly man that I knew.

His routine was the same each day: rising, preparing himself meticulously, as though he was going to work— calisthenics, pressed shirt and trousers, impeccable grooming—just to go downstairs, eat and then take his seat in the office downstairs, directly below his bedroom. As a child, I noticed that he was the only adult in the house who did not go out to work in the morning. 'Work' was something for which people wore uniforms or carried special tools: the nurse's crisp starched hat, and the doctor's bag, suit jackets and pleated skirts, the school teacher's satchels filled with corrected exercise books.

And always the great hurry in the morning to get out of the house. The dignity of work was generated in the mysterious rituals adults performed in those sunrise hours, as a tightly wound energy that unravelled itself throughout the working day.

What did it mean, the short commute of my grandfather from upstairs to downstairs? That becoming a pensioner meant that he no longer participated in the troubles of adults making their way in the world?

When I was lucky enough to sit with grandfather in his office—he at his big desk with his correspondence, and me at a smaller improvised one in the corner near the encyclopaedias, with my little notebooks—I would get a real education. Most days he received visitors, many of whom were women from the neighbourhood. After elaborate greetings at the front door, the visitors would be ushered into the office and I would be ushered out. Eventually, the doors would open again, and my grandfather would lead them to the garage at the back of the back of the house, where there were straw-coloured woven bags of dry goods such as millet, rice, beans, and sometime fresh vegetables, and he or his assistant would dip out measuring cups of the foodstuffs into smaller bags for the visitors. The visitors left with their food, and back in the office Joseph recorded the transactions in a ledger.

My grandfather was running a food cooperative out of our home. In the 1980s, the policies of the World Bank and International Monetary

SHAME! and Masculinity

Fund squeezed African states, and other postcolonial states, to their breaking points. Currencies were devalued overnight. 'Structural adjustment' meant that austerity ruled the day, with cuts in funding to education, social services, health and social welfare. In Nigeria basic foodstuffs became ridiculously expensive: an egg was a luxury. In this climate of utter devaluation, new forms of shame entered daily life in the Nigerian post-colony. One of the most severe forms of shame arises from the inability to feed oneself and one's family. This is the shame that licks at the edges of most people's working lives. This is the shame palpable in the rituals and procedures of charities, welfare offices and bureaucracies everywhere. Joseph would have gained intimate, bodily knowledge of this during his working years, in his journeys into the agricultural interior of Western Nigeria.

As an adult I now understand that what Joseph had designed in our home was a small yet efficient way for mitigating the shame produced by a global system of devaluing human life and labour. In the process of greeting of visitors at the front door and their private meetings in his office and the trips to the garage, a deeply isolating shame was transformed into the bonds of neighbourliness. Stories of privation were shared with a neighbour, without the need to justify the value of one's work, or one's life, to an indifferent social welfare system. The food cooperative was local, for everyone within walking distance. It was pay-as-you-go. Those who could pay subsidized those who could not, and the prices were low and fair, already a magical feat in a world economic system that turned rice and eggs into unattainable luxuries, and delivered devalued currencies in exchange for backbreaking work.

Food was the province of women. Women would be the ones who normally did the buying and selling of food. Women would normally be the ones who faced the hunger of their households, who would have to stretch a bag of rice for a month. That was a form of shame many men could not face. Of course, women would be the ones most likely to visit my grandfather's office. For me, Joseph's food cooperative was an education in what good a certain kind of masculinity could do in the world. His way of leadership was to extend the dignity of his body, his home, his office to others. His gift was to face the shame of others and not run from it, leaving his neighbours in isolation. In my grandfather's office, this domestic shame could be shared and transformed in a small way.

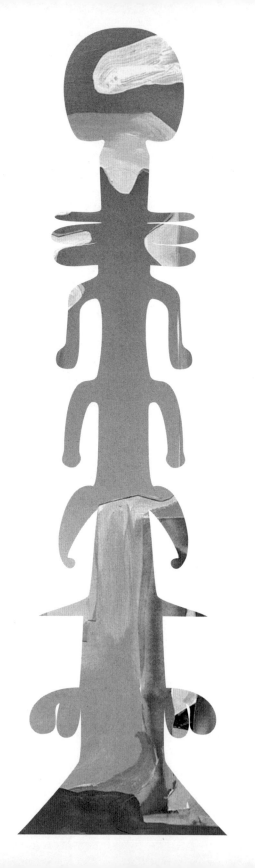

THINKING ABOUT THE SONIC TRIGGERS FOR *SPECIAL BOY*

Philip Miller

Sparky was a boy who didn't like to practice the piano. But one day while struggling to practise, the piano comes to life and asks him to run his fingers over the keys. Sparky does exactly that and with one rather flourishing 'glissando' he magically starts to play like a great virtuoso. This was my favourite moment in *Sparky's Magic Piano*, a recording which I listened to over and over again on the turntable in my parents' living room when I was a boy of seven years old. It was 1973.

Both Sparky's stern piano teacher and rather over-anxious mother are thrilled with his extraordinary transformation into a child prodigy and they book gigs for him at all the famous concert halls across America. After playing Rachmaninov's *Piano Sonata in C sharp Minor* to rapturous applause at Carnegie Hall in New York, the most prestigious of all his concerts, the piano unexpectedly lets him down at the encore. It literally stops playing for him. Poor Sparky is left banging away at the keys, desperately ashamed. Through the cacophony, we hear his mother's gentle, assuring voice, cutting through his panicked state of mind as if it were a living nightmare. Suddenly, together with Sparky, we realize what is going on. Sparky's mother is waking him up. It was all just a bad dream. The story had a moral to it: Sparky agrees to practise more often, if he is to succeed to be a great pianist. Looking back as an adult, the story's message was rather heavy-handed. It was to encourage children who played musical instruments to practise daily. Sparky's fate tells children that there are no short cuts to becoming an accomplished virtuoso pianist other than through hard graft—a message that today fits comfortably with Malcolm Gladwell's 'tipping point' theory!

In 2008, I found, on the web, a CD of *Sparky's Magic Piano*. I recognized the cover art immediately: a rather kitschy, 1950s stylized drawing of Sparky, a young boy with rosy cherubic cheeks, golden curly locks covering a head too large for the rest of his body. Sitting at the piano, on his stool, his one hand is raised rather flamboyantly in the air whilst the fingers of his other hand are touching the keys. The piano which he is playing is animated, wickedly winking at Sparky: his partner in crime. As a boy, I was fascinated by this image of Sparky. It was both repellent but also curiously compelling. His big head mimicked my own, already the reason for much bullying and jeering: I was called 'Lolly-head' (a lolly is a frozen sucker).

Listening to the story for the first time in at least thirty years, I was struck by the emotions that the voices and music and album cover triggered in me. My experiences of being bullied, and feeling ashamed of my nascent

Album design: Jo Ractliffe

Special Boy, album design

feelings of being attracted to men, came flooding back.

Sound triggers nostalgia—and pathos. But something else was happening too. I was not just reliving those childhood experiences, I had adult perspectives on them. This was the catalyst for a new sonic imagination, the result of which you are experiencing now, in *Special Boy.*

Like Sparky, I was 'A Special Boy'. When I discovered Sparky, I was already a 'swot' and a 'prodigy' and spent hours every day after school at the piano. My life, in fact, mirrored the relationship that Sparky had with his talking piano. Sparky had made an inanimate instrument come to life, talk to him and be his friend. My piano was also my best friend and companion. I could run my hands over its keys and it would voice my loneliness as a young boy. In my sonic imagination of romantic 'Chopin

Nocturnes and Schubert Impromptus', I could escape from my fears of being bullied. I could be that fabulously famous concert pianist, loved and fêted by everyone.

But at my school in Cape Town, playing the piano was for girls, or effeminate boys, no good at sports. It was an admission that I was different, and no amount of brilliance at the keyboard could take away my self-hatred and shame. My classmates would call me a 'moffie', which in South African slang, is pejorative and means a queer, a faggot, an effeminate man. There are several different explanations put forward for this word's derivation but the one I like the best is that it derives from the Afrikaans word, 'mofskaap': castrated sheep! I grew to fear even the sound of the word—those two syllables 'mof-fie' (/ˈmɒfi/). When boys in the classroom or gymnasium used it, I would feel myself shrinking into my seat, lowering my head. The word felt like a stone aimed right at me.

Sparky's voice was high-pitched, even shrill, like that of a little girl, I thought. With feelings of self-loathing and shame, I started to hear myself as speaking differently from the other boys at school—a bit like Sparky. Did I have a 'gay voice'? Did my voice betray me and signify to everyone that I was queer? I was told by my class English teacher that I read out loud very well and that my enunciation was excellent, as close as possible to the 'Queen's English' considering I was a young boy growing up in a former colony in Africa. Was this then my problem: that I spoke too posh and my voice sounded too nasal? Or was it the overall timbre? Too gentle and languid? Too many sibilant 's's? Too many drawn out vowels and too few short-clipped consonants?

My repulsion at the sound of my voice continued through school into adulthood. To this day I become irrationally irate if someone mistakes my voice for a 'woman' on the phone. When I was thinking about how I would work with Sparky, I remembered that there was a recording of my voice, age thirteen, practising my Bar Mitzvah speech. I am a hoarder, and I went to find the shoe box in the back of my cupboard with all my Bar Mitzvah paraphernalia: congratulatory telegrams, Bar Mitzvah cards, a pin that kept my prayer shawl neatly together, and even a detailed list of all the presents I received. One of the

BAR MITZVAH MEMORIES

Special Boy, details, photo: Sue Kramer

cards said, 'You are a Special Boy today' and it forms part of this installation.

My Aunt Rhona and Uncle Louis had given me a Sony TC-55 portable cassette recorder for my Bar Mitzvah, so that I could record myself playing my own compositions on the piano. I started doing this immediately, in the week leading up to the celebrations. This was my first recording device, and I was so excited that I wanted to record everything I could hear around me. This, I imagine, is how I came to record my rehearsal of my Bar Mitzvah speech, which I now found preserved for posterity on a cassette tape in the box, along with the handwritten speech itself.

I still owned a cassette recorder, so I could digitally make a transfer on CD. Listening to my recorded child-voice was incredibly difficult. This was, largely, because my father died soon after my Bar Mitzvah, and it brought back those memories. But it was also because even though my adult self could recognize that I sounded just like any boy just before puberty— his voice not yet having broken— a child-part of myself connected, once more, to those feelings of self-loathing and shame. I decided I needed to capture this, and this is why I have recorded my own 'adult

Philip Miller

man-voice' in the new soundscape, sometimes mimicking and at other times in sync with, the little boy Sparky's voice. This disruption feels like a reclamation, a re-appropriation of the slurs for my own creative use. I was startled by how therapeutic it was for me, to scream 'MOFFIE!' into the microphone.

I also sing the word 'moffie' to the musical motif of the talking piano, using the same Sonovox effect that was used to make the piano's voice in *Sparky's Magic Piano*. Nowadays you use a software plug-in known as a 'Vocoder'. I loved this strange peculiar electronic timbre of the talking piano and when I started to research the sound material of *Special Boy* I discovered that the talking piano's voice was created using this effect, invented by Gilbert Wright in 1939. The original Sonovox was a rather crude electronic device using small transducers, which were attached to the throat of the person singing or talking and would pick up the voice sounds and turn them into electronic impulses. In my background reading around the history of the recording of *Sparky's Magic Piano*, I read that early childhood educators have opined that the piano's voice was far too disturbing for young children. That deep male

Sparky's Magic Piano, record, photo: Sue Kramer

voice, warped into a tone that now seems quite camp but that aroused in my child-self a feeling of danger, erotic excitement, and concealment. I understood that Sparky had to keep his friendship with his talking piano a secret in order not to be found out as a phoney and a fake. With the help of his piano, he pretended to everyone else that he was a star rather than a 'moffie'. Of course, the piano stops playing, for no reason. Was this an early imprint of abandonment, of what I imagined might happen to me, as a queer, looking for love?

Writing this text has made me recognize that my re-appropriation of these two potent recordings from my own personal archive, has triggered in me a new perception or way of remembering my past—carrying the memory into the present. It gave me a chance to engage with my feelings and emotions from childhood, as an adult, re-telling the story as I worked to produce a different sound world, a different narrative, for the listener.

QR code for Special Boy:
https://vimeo.com/436896055

SHAME, ENVY, IMPASSE AND HOPE
The Psychopolitics of Violence in South Africa

Wahbie Long

Introduction

In her celebrated collection of letters, Madame de Sévigné would detail the hangings, quarterings, and wheelings of seventeenth-century France. On one occasion—the execution of a peasant—De Sévigné witnessed the condemned man's terror at his imminent death. He shivered and wailed, his body wriggling in the hangman's noose—a spectacle for the ladies and gentlemen gathered that morning. And yet De Sévigné was troubled: she could not fathom why a commoner should be so horrified at the prospect of his own death.[1] She was not a particularly vicious woman— on the contrary, she was 'a rich human creature of balance and sanity',[2] described as 'delicious'[3] by those who knew her. But in the words of Alexis de Tocqueville, 'Madame de Sévigné had no clear notion of suffering in any one who was not a person of quality'.[4]

One may interpret the madame's indifference as a historical artefact— the age of Enlightenment had not yet begun. In the mind of the aristocrat, it made perfect sense to treat the masses with a brutality that matched their supposedly brutish souls. It would fall to the humanists of the eighteenth century to formulate a belief in the dignity of 'man'—albeit 'man' of a certain hue. But in the intervening centuries, that belief has evolved into something we can all appreciate today: the idea that *all* human beings deserve to be treated with dignity. In his new book on identity, Francis Fukuyama goes as far as positing the

1. Richard Sennett and Jonathan Cobb, *The Hidden Injuries of Class* (London: Faber & Faber, 1972).

2. Gamaliel Bradford, 'Portrait of a Lady: Madame de Sévigné', *Sewanee Review* 23, no. 1 (1915), pp. 36–48, here p. 37.

3. Ibid., p. 41.

4. Alexis de Tocqueville, *Democracy in America, Vol. 2*, trans. H. Reeve, p. 151 (London: Longmans, 1889, orig. published 1835).

universal existence of something the ancient Greeks called *thymos*—'the part of the soul that craves recognition of dignity'.[5] Human beings, that is, seek recognition from their peers, and when they do not receive it, one of two things happens. If they feel undervalued, they become resentful, and if they reckon within themselves a failure to meet the standards of others, they feel ashamed. Human beings are not satisfied with only food and shelter: they also want respect.

In this chapter, I am concerned mainly with the question of dignity. My general position is that shame and envy—when framed at the societal level—are not only among the principal *drivers* of violence in South Africa, they are also *responses* to violence in the broadest sense of the term, that is, violence as '[a] manifestation of power that denies people their humanity'.[6] In support of this position, I offer three interlocking arguments. First, I contend that the poor and working classes respond to the shame inflicted on them by *structural* violence with a scarcely believable interpersonal violence of their own—directed against their own. Second, I suggest that the black aspiring middle class—the intellectual elite specifically—responds to *symbolic* violence by means of a reaction formation, an unconscious *ressentiment* according to Max Scheler's rendition of that term.[7] And third—following Alexandre Kojève's influential reading of Hegel— I maintain that many white South Africans are mired in an existential

5. Francis Fukuyama, *Identity: Contemporary Identity Politics and the Struggle for Recognition* (London: Profile Books, 2018).

6. Stuart Henry, 'What Is School Violence? An Integrated Definition', *Annals of the American Academy of Political and Social Science* 567 (2000), pp. 16–29, here p. 20.

7. Max Scheler, *Ressentiment*, trans. W.W. Holdheim (New York: Free Press, 1961, orig. published 1915).

impasse that blocks reciprocal recognition, and that they have settled for lives of alienated consumption instead. Finally, I consider the implications of widespread shame, envy, and impasse in this land of terrible beauty—as Yeats might have put it—for the cultivation of life-giving hope.

Shame
The history books tell us that much of twentieth-century politics was driven by economic issues: the left focused on workers, unions and social democratic goals, while the right called for small government and free enterprise. In the twenty-first century, however, the political spectrum has constellated itself around markers of social difference: today, both the left and right advocate on behalf of groups they consider marginalized, be they women, black people, the white working class, or nationalists. It is not that class politics has become irrelevant to cultural politics—what appears to have happened, rather, is that the politics of equality has been dissociated from the politics of difference in both public and intellectual life.

SHAME! and Masculinity

8. Nancy Fraser and Axel Honneth, *Redistribution or Recognition? A Political-philosophical Exchange* (London: Verso, 2003).

9. Fukuyama, *Identity*.

10. Ibid.

11. Hussein A. Bulhan, *Frantz Fanon and the Psychology of Oppression* (New York: Plenum Press, 1985).

12. Frantz Fanon, *Racism and Culture*, in *The Fanon Reader*, ed. A. Haddour, pp. 19–29 (London: Pluto Press, 2006, orig. published 1956), p. 26.

The Marxist feminist Nancy Fraser identifies these two camps as the politics of *redistribution* and the politics of *recognition*, respectively. She describes how the concept of redistribution is rooted in liberal politics whereas the notion of recognition draws heavily on Hegel's phenomenology of consciousness.[8] In the public imagination, talk of redistribution is equated with *class* politics while recognition discourse is reduced usually to *identity* politics, which involves struggles over categories such as gender, 'race', sexuality and so on. What will interest us as psychologists is that the dominant political trend of our times—identity politics—is profoundly psychological, being organized around the injured dignity of oppressed groups. Each group, that is, claims an internal group identity that has been rejected by the outside world. For proponents of identity politics, therefore, the problem of dignity turns on a society that is pathologically unvalidating. Human beings are first and foremost social beings, and when social formations compromise the dignity of marginalized groups, the consequences can be devastating, involving either self-hating shame or envious resentment. For Hegel, therefore, the history of our species is a history of the struggle for recognition.[9] Human beings only become conscious of themselves when recognized by others, and the failure to attain this recognition must eventuate in conflict. History begins, therefore, with warriors who risk their lives in order to compel their adversaries to recognize them.[10] If they succeed, they become masters who are recognized without having to reciprocate, but if they fail, they become slaves who must recognize their vanquishers without themselves being recognized.[11] Inside this matrix of unreciprocated recognition, Hegel's famous master-slave dialectic takes shape, the master affirmed in his dignity and the slave deprived of his humanity.

It goes without saying that the history of South Africa is a history of masters and slaves. Over the course of three centuries, European settlers subdued the native populations, confiscating their lands and exploiting their labour. It did not suffice, however, that the locals were defeated militarily and economically: the entire edifice of their cultural traditions had to be liquidated. Material domination, therefore, went hand in hand with ideological domination—and in the South African instance, that meant the denigration and shaming of all black people. Frantz Fanon explains how, in the colonial encounter, '[i]t is not possible to enslave men without logically making them inferior through and through'.[12] Henceforth, the native population looks on helplessly as the occupying powers set about obliterating its cultural forms, imposing 'a pejorative judgment with respect to its original forms of existing'.[13] The natives are not recognized as human, being nothing more than an afterthought in virgin land. They live in

> [a] world divided into compartments, a motionless, Manichaeistic world, a world of statues: the statue of the general who carried out the conquest, the statue of the engineer who built the bridge; a world which is sure of itself, which crushes with its stones the backs flayed by whips: this is the colonial world.[14]

A catastrophe of such magnitude can mean only one thing—that 'God is not on [their] side'.[15]

Fearing death, the black man is '[s]ealed into that crushing object-hood… For not only *must* [he] be black; he must be black in relation to the white man… [He] has no ontological resistance…'[16] He simply is what the white man says he must be. Feelings of inferiority and shame overwhelm him[17] but he never stops desiring the world of the master:[18] 'For the black man there is only one destiny. And it is white. Long ago the black man admitted the unarguable superiority of the white man, and all his efforts are aimed at achieving a white exis-tence.'[19] This should not surprise us: the black man has no option but to *lactify* himself, having witnessed the wholesale

13. Ibid., p. 25.

14. Frantz Fanon, *The Wretched of the Earth* (London: Penguin, 2001, orig. published 1963), p. 40.

15. Fanon, *Racism and Culture*, p. 25.

16. Frantz Fanon, *Black Skin, White Masks* (London: Pluto Press, 2008, orig. published 1952), pp. 82–83, emphasis added.

17. Fanon, *Racism and Culture*, p. 25.

18. Fanon, *The Wretched of the Earth*, p. 41.

19. Fanon, *Black Skin, White Masks*, p. 178.

20. Fanon, *The Wretched of the Earth*, p. 40.

destruction of his former mode of being. The problem of course is that the border between the black and white worlds is impregnable:

> The native is a being hemmed in; apartheid is simply one form of the division into compartments of the colonial world. The first thing which the native learns is to stay in his place, and not to go beyond certain limits.[20]

The black man, accordingly, is released from his fetters only while he sleeps; he dreams constantly of physical prowess, Fanon claims, in a classic case of wish fulfilment. On returning to waking life, the wish is denied once more. Like Aesop's fox reaching for the grapes, the black man can never be white for that would mean being recognized as human.

Disrespect rains down on the black subject. Unable to resolve the existential dilemma, the shame

SHAME! and Masculinity

21. June P. Tangney et al., 'Relation of Shame and Guilt to Constructive Versus Destructive Responses to Anger across the Lifespan', *Journal of Personality & Social Psychology* 70, no. 4 (2006), pp. 797–809.

22. Fanon, *The Wretched of the Earth*, p. 40.

23. Sennett, *The Hidden Injuries of Class*, p. 22.

24. Philippe Bourgeois, 'The Power of Violence in War and Peace: Post-Cold War Lessons from El Salvador', *Ethnography* 2, no. 1 (2001), pp. 5–34.

25. Léon Wurmser, 'The Superego as Herald of Resentment', *Psychoanalytic Inquiry* 29, no. 5 (2009), pp. 386–410, here pp. 396–397.

26. See Hoosen Coovadia et al., 'The Health and Health System of South Africa: Historical Roots of Current Public Health Challenges', *Lancet* 374 (2009), pp. 817–834; also, Mohamed Seedat et al., 'Violence and Injuries in South Africa: Prioritising an Agenda for Prevention', *Lancet*, 374 (2009), pp. 1011–1022.

27. Wahbie Long, 'Essence or Experience? A New Direction for African Psychology', *Theory & Psychology* 27, no. 3 (2017), pp. 293–312.

28. Richard Wilkinson and Kate Pickett, *The Spirit Level: Why Equality is Better for Everyone* (London: Penguin, 2010).

becomes unbearable. The resentment towards the self is turned outwards in an attempt to restore a sense of agency eroded by shame.[21] Soon enough, it erupts into senseless violence—but not against the oppressor. Instead, the victims of structural violence will vent their rage first against themselves, their violence so incomprehensible that—in the words of Fanon—'the police and magistrates do not know which way to turn'.[22] According to sociologist Richard Sennett, poverty encourages 'chaotic, arbitrary, and unpredictable behaviour' as it prevents people from 'act[ing] rationally and exercis[ing] self-control'.[23] The shame of deprivation and the burning sense of injustice that goes with it undermine the legitimacy of the law in the eyes of the disenfranchised. Mindless violence breaks out as resentment towards the power establishment is displaced onto substitutes: women, children, refugees and—especially—other black men. What ethnographers call 'everyday violence' starts to set in: the routinization of interpersonal aggression at the microlevel and the constitution during peacetime of a virtual 'common-sense of violence'.[24]

Displaced from its original object, the experience of bitterness explodes into the external world as spontaneous, sadistic, and often arbitrary violence[25]—a process borne out by statistics on violence in post-apartheid South Africa.[26] For example, the national rate of violent deaths is five times the global average. The murder of women is six times the world average. The raw numbers confirm that most victims are black while the highest rates are suffered by coloured men and women. What we know about homicide hotspots is that Cape Town ranks fourteenth in the world and—by some distance—first in Africa.[27] Nationally, an estimated half-a-million rapes are perpetrated against women and girls every year. Outbreaks of xenophobic violence occur with regularity. Meanwhile, income inequality and male youth unemployment emerge as the strongest correlates of murder and major assault. In their widely praised book, *The Spirit Level*, epidemiologists Richard Wilkinson and Kate Pickett describe how inequality in modern, industrialized nations generates fear, envy, and resentment, affecting the physical and mental wellbeing of both the poor and the well-to-do.[28]

Feelings of shame, that is, are difficult to escape in class society. As Norbert Elias observes, the ubiquity of class contempt dictates that even young children intuit social stratification long before they acquire any understanding of it.[29] In fact, the political conditions most conducive for the shaming of poor and working-class people are liberal bourgeois democracies, which are shot through with invidious cultures of social comparison. Democratic South Africa, that is, aggravates the psychological torture of its citizens: they live in a constitutional dispensation that guarantees the equality of all yet they feel themselves barred from enjoying its material benefits. Social *ressentiment*—in the words of Scheler—'must therefore be strongest in a society like ours, where… formal social equality, publicly recognized, go[es] hand in hand with wide factual differences in power, property, and education'.[30] For ordinary people, such a divergence can only make sense by evaluating themselves negatively. By admitting that they lack all 'badges of ability',[31] the poor man and woman can lay to rest the question that has followed them all their lives: the question of why—despite their best efforts—they got nowhere in life. Assuming personal responsibility for a society that failed them, not only do they feel the pain of inadequacy—they resent themselves for feeling it.

But the injustice of it all does not end there. For those who believe they *do* possess a badge of ability, powerful sanctions will be levied against them should they ever resolve to wear it.[32] Consider, for example, the case of a school for working-class children.[33] The teachers are anxious to enforce

29. Norbert Elias, *The Civilizing Process: Sociogenetic and Psychogenetic Investigations* (Malden: Blackwell, 2000).

30. Scheler, *Ressentiment*, p. 28.

31. Sennett, *The Hidden Injuries of Class*, p. 62.

32. See Ron Suskind, *A Hope in the Unseen: An American Odyssey From the Inner City to the Ivy League* (New York: Broadway Books, 1998).

33. Sennett, *The Hidden Injuries of Class*, pp. 79–90.

discipline; they imagine that their charges do not value order and routine, given their unruly backgrounds. The general mass is deemed unteachable while one or two are singled out as having potential. The few who are made to stand out, must make an agonizing decision: excel and shame their peers—for which they will be bullied mercilessly—or, accept the shaming of their teachers, but enjoy the bonds of friendship. An identical scenario faces the worker who may harbour fantasies of excellence: get promoted to supervisor and earn the scorn of your colleagues, or live with them as equals, sharing the common bond of indignity. It is no wonder that the few who rise above their class cannot live with the shame of having distinguished themselves. They can neither be who they are nor stay where they are: many will marry outside their circle; most will leave the neighbourhood for good.

That is how class society operates: 'In turning people against each other, the class system of authority and judgment-making goes itself into

SHAME! and Masculinity

34. Ibid., p. 150.

35. Jonathan Burns, 'The Mental Health Gap in South Africa: A Human Rights Issue', *Equal Rights Review* 6 (2011), pp, 99–113.

36. Seedat et al., *Violence and Injuries in South Africa*, p. 1015.

37. Burns, *The Mental Health Gap in South Africa*, p. 102.

38. Sandro Galea, Arijit Nandi, and David Vlahov, 'The Social Epidemiology of Substance Use', *Epidemiologic Reviews* 26, no. 1 (2004), pp. 36–52.

39. See Ronda L. Dearing, Jeffrey Stuewig, and June Price Tangney, 'On the Importance of Distinguishing Shame from Guilt: Relations to Problematic Alcohol and Drug Use', *Addictive Behaviors* 30, no. 7 (2005), pp. 1392–1404; also, Shelley A. Wiechelt, 'The Specter of Shame in Substance Misuse', *Substance Use & Misuse* 42, no. 2–3 (2007), pp. 399–409.

40. Manfred S. Frings, 'Introduction', in Scheler, *Ressentiment*, pp. 1–18.

hiding; the system is left unchallenged as people enthralled by the enigmas of its power battle one another for respect.'[34] In an unequal society that professes equality for all, shame rears its head at every turn; for the poor and working classes in particular, substance use becomes a ready consolation. Indeed, South Africa—which has the second highest Gini coefficient for income inequality in the world[35]— also has one of the highest alcohol consumptions in the world.[36] Alcohol abuse, in turn, is strongly related to the perpetration of acts of violence and, according to the United Nations Office on Drugs and Crime, our country has the fourth highest rate of drug-related offences in the world.[37] Although the value of socioeconomic status as a predictor of substance use is contested,[38] a growing body of research suggests that the relationship between addiction and *shame*—as distinct from guilt—is mutually reinforcing.[39] Resorting to substances, that is, can be conceptualized as a defence against chronic feelings of shame—as much as it can trigger the very same feelings.

Ressentiment

The Spanish philosopher José Ortega y Gasset once wrote of his German counterpart Max Scheler that he was 'the first man [sic] of genius, the Adam of the new Paradise'. Scheler was widely regarded as one of the most brilliant minds of the twentieth century but, with his unexpected death in 1928 and the suppression of his work by the Nazis, his ideas faded rapidly.[40] I want to resurrect one of Scheler's ideas today, namely, his reading of the concept ressentiment as laid out in his book, *The Role of Ressentiment in the Make-Up of Morals*. The concept was not originally his own: the first to elaborate ressentiment systematically was in fact Nietzsche, who decried the Christian values of love, compassion, and humility as a form of slave morality. For Nietzsche, what lay at the heart of Christian ethics was, effectively, a reaction formation: the early Christians were motivated by impotence, hatred, and envy of their Roman masters—and they sought to reverse their lowliness by supplanting Roman morality with a value system of their own. Acknowledging his debt to his countryman, Scheler quotes as follows from Nietzsche's *Genealogy of Morals*:

The inoffensiveness of the weak, even the cowardice in which he is rich, his unavoidable obligation to wait at the door acquires a good name, as 'patience', it is also called virtue; the inability to avenge oneself is supposed to be a voluntary renunciation of revenge, sometimes it is even called forgiveness... They also speak of 'love for one's enemies'—and they sweat while doing so.[41]

41. Scheler, *Ressentiment*, p. 45.

42. Lewis B. Coser, 'Max Scheler: An Introduction', in Scheler, *Ressentiment*, pp. 5–36, here p. 14.

43. Ibid., p. 47.

44. Ibid., p. 64.

When approached through a social justice paradigm, Scheler's book is likely to offend: several commentators have even suggested that his work was a massive projection of his own *ressentiment* at the social leveling of the early twentieth century. His thinking was 'deeply aristocratic' and his endorsement of social and value hierarchies meant that, for Scheler, inequality was a natural feature of human existence.[42] On the other hand, the rise of what Fukuyama calls 'the politics of resentment' has transformed Scheler's *ressentiment* into a potentially valuable tool for analyzing the latest trend in local and global politics—identity politics—which threatens to shatter all possibilities for mutual recognition and reconciliation. It is towards Scheler's own treatment of *ressentiment* that I now turn.

In their efforts to preserve the specialized meaning of the term, Scheler's translators prefer the French *ressentiment* over the English 'resentment'. This is because Scheler himself has in mind something much deeper than 'mere' resentment. In his view, *ressentiment* has several elements. First, a human being experiences some injury and an associated negative emotion. Second, he or she is unable to express this emotion directly, usually on account of occupying a lower position in a given status hierarchy. Third, the negative emotion is consequently repressed. And fourth, under the direction of a repressed desire for revenge that proceeds 'via rancor, envy, and impulse to detract all the way to spite',[43] the subject engages in value delusions and their corresponding judgments, demeaning values that are objectively superior while venerating those that are objectively inferior.

These are the essentials of Scheler's *ressentiment,* the practical meaning of which is best illustrated through examples—and Scheler himself provides several. The priest, for one, is a typical *ressentiment* subject: he is required to control his emotions and project himself as the embodiment of serenity. Then there is the mother-in-law who must not only relinquish her son to another woman but must 'offer her congratulations, and receive the intruder with affection'.[44] Scheler reports a case of what he calls class ressentiment—specifically, an incident in 1912 near Berlin when someone tied a length of wire between two trees on either side of the road so that drivers passing through would be decapitated. What unites Scheler's collection of *ressentiment* characters is a 'way of

45. Ibid., p. 67, original emphasis.

46. James Martel, 'Walter Benjamin', in *Histories of Violence: Post-war Critical Thought*, ed. Bradd Evans and Terrell Carver, pp. 14–30 (London: Zed Books, 2017), here pp. 21–25.

47. Pierre Bourdieu, 'Social Space and Symbolic Power', *Sociological Theory* 7, no. 1 (1989), pp. 14–25, here p. 24.

48. Fanon, *Black Skin, White Masks*, p. 117.

thinking which attributes creative power to mere *negation* and *criticism*'.[45]

Reaction Formation

This preliminary account of *ressentiment* brings me to the second leg of my argument, which is an analysis of the black intellectual elite's response to the *symbolic violence* that pervades institutions of higher learning in South Africa. I do so partly in an attempt to understand a phenomenon in which my own working life is immersed but primarily to draw attention to the pervasiveness of envious resentment in our public life. According to sociologist Pierre Bourdieu, symbolic violence designates the intimate encounter in which the oppressed cannot help but assess their predicament through the terms of reference provided by the oppressor and thereby participate unwittingly in their own subjugation. The protests that have shaken university campuses over the last four years, that is, signal a conscientization about the workings of symbolic violence. All the talk of intellectual colonization, Eurocentrism, whiteness, privilege, epistemic violence and so on is

university-speak for a perceived system of knowledge and an encompassing institutional culture that make it impossible for black students and academics to participate as their white counterparts' equals in intellectual life. Their argument is that the dice are loaded—that the rules of the game prevent them from challenging the ideological workings of the knowledge-making apparatus. Unable to challenge the system from the inside, they seek therefore to disrupt, their seemingly incoherent demands an example of Walter Benjamin's notion of 'pure means' as a response to capitalist violence.[46] Straightforward enough—except that, for anyone who believes in the existence of the unconscious, 'the simple is never but the simplified', in the words of Gaston Bachelard.[47]

Recall Fanon's reluctant admission in the opening pages of *Black Skin, White Masks*—that the only real destiny for black people is the colour white. The psychological import of Fanon's verdict cannot be overestimated because it raises the crucial question of how—in the minds of student protesters—the pursuit of whiteness is transformed into its denigration. Freudian theory offers an elegant solution, namely, the 'reaction formation'. As per Fanon, the black subject desires to be white. There is no fear of whiteness *per se*—but there is an overwhelming fear of the *desire* for whiteness. It is no longer the black subject but the white subject who becomes—in the words of Fanon— 'a phobogenic object, a stimulus to anxiety'.[48] Whiteness is converted into a phobia: 'We can't breathe!' the Fallists[49] exclaim, expressing one of the classic symptoms of a panic attack. The deprecation of whiteness, in other words, attenuates the very desire for it.[50]

Political commentators suggest that Fallist fury has a touch of drama to it, that they doth protest too much. Adam Habib, for example, has written about the 'politics of spectacle', which he interprets as a strategy used by minority factions to seize control of the political narrative on campus.[51] I would go further by suggesting that the *performative* aspect of Fallism is typical of reaction formations, which are habitually overelaborate and affected.[52] Moreover, the implacability of student anger has an almost compulsive feel to it—another characteristic of the reaction formation—for no matter how far backwards university management bent, students could never feel satisfied. It was as if they *had* to be angry—regardless of the actual deal on the negotiating table.

Envy

Reaction formations aside, why does the wish for whiteness inspire such anxiety? It is here that the Kleinian theory of envy proves instructive. According to the standard version,

envy is constitutional and enters the world with the neonate. The infant revels in gratification at the mother's nourishing breast but also has to contend with deprivation. It is this latter experience that generates the persecutory anxiety of the paranoid-schizoid position. The infant starts to hate the good breast and—as is also the case with gratification—spoils it with envy.[53] Sadistic attacks on the breast increase until it is entirely without value: in the words of Klein, 'it has become bad by being bitten up and poisoned by urine and faeces'.[54] The stronger and more enduring the envy, the more difficult it becomes for the infant to reclaim the lost object; the ego becomes fragile and the

49. 'The idea of Fallism first emerged as a collective noun to describe student movements at universities in South Africa that use the "Must Fall" hashtag, including #RhodesMustFall (#RMF) and #FeesMustFall. These Fallist movements argue that the university's epistemic architecture is deeply rooted in coloniality, and that consequently, the university as we know it, must fall.' Kayum Ahmed. Retrieved from: https://blog.apaonline.org/2019/03/19/on-black-pain-black-liberation-and-the-rise-of-fallism/.

50. See Calvin S. Hall, *A Primer of Freudian Psychology* (New York: World Publishing Company, 1954), p. 92.

51. Adam Habib, *The Politics of Spectacle: Reflections on the 2016 Student Protests*, 5 December 2016. Retrieved from www.dailymaverick.co.za/article/2016-12-05-op-ed-the-politics-of-spectacle-reflections-on-the-2016-student-protests/.

52. Hall, *A Primer of Freudian Psychology*, p. 92.

53. Melanie Klein, *Envy and Gratitude and Other Works 1946–1963* (New York: Free Press, 1975), pp. 183–187.

54. Ibid., p. 186.

∩ALI∩I MALA∩I
Asifa

2020, animation, iPad drawings

55. Donna M. Orange, *Emotional Understanding: Studies in Psychoanalytic Epistemology* (New York: Guilford Press, 1995), pp. 99–104.

56. Ibid.

57. Paul Hoggett, 'Ressentiment and Grievance', *British Journal of Psychotherapy*, 34, no. 3 (2018), pp. 393–407. See citation of Freud (1921) on p. 400.

58. Simon Clarke, 'The Concept of Envy: Primitive Drives, Social Encounters and Ressentiment', *Psychoanalysis, Culture & Society* 9, no. 1 (2004), pp. 105–17. See citation of Segal (1989) on p. 108.

capacity for love and hope fades into obscurity.

Whereas Klein conceived of envy as an expression of the death drive, I want to approach it primarily as an intersubjective phenomenon,[55] as a destructive mode of being resulting from persistently unequal social encounters. Viewed from this perspective, the relevance of Kleinian theory for a psychological analysis of Fallism becomes obvious upon recognizing the equivalence of elite institutions with the nourishing breast. The University of Cape Town, for example, dispenses precious knowledge, financial support, networking opportunities and—above all—the promise of a life of dignity.

But for Fallists, the internal logic of the institution is 'white'. They feel themselves deprived of the fruits they imagined a university education would confer, which triggers for many the familiar feeling of deprivation. They feel persecuted by an institution experienced as massively shaming, and as they begin to compare themselves to more privileged students, their shame turns to envy.[56] In a literal display of anal sadism, they set about spoiling the university, unloading bins of human faeces into lecture halls. Haunted by a relentless sense of grievance, they set fire to life-affirming artworks and shut down life-giving classes of knowledge. 'If we cannot enjoy this place, then no one will', they may as well be saying. It does not matter that they may be damaging their own university— at least in the short run. As Freud observes, '[I]f one cannot be the favourite oneself, at all events nobody else shall be the favourite… [S]ocial justice means that we deny ourselves many things so that others may have to do without them as well.'[57]

But this is a somewhat pragmatic assessment next to the psychological calculus that is now in play: the more the Fallists destroy the institution, the more impoverished the collective ego feels. Their envy grows stronger still and the protests spiral out of control.[58]

The experience of deprivation and the destruction of the good object unleash a merciless persecutory anxiety; paranoia, aggression and projection take over as the dominant psychological themes in university life.[59] With the good object now spoilt, it becomes impossible to distinguish the good from the bad[60] as the Fallists start agitating for the decolonization of the curriculum. The entire Enlightenment canon—they believe—must be dismantled because it stands for colonization by intellectual means. They insist that the Enlightenment values, ideals, and methods that came out of Western Europe are simply unworkable in the South African context. Reason itself becomes the object of their opprobrium—even science must fall—as *lived experience* emerges as the new basis for argumentation. The purported universals of the Enlightenment project are regarded as invalid in relation to the particulars found in the colonized world. A decolonial form of praxis is sought that will privilege the lived experiences of the oppressed here and around the world.

With the Fallists attempting to replace one set of academic values with another that must yet be determined, Scheler's *ressentiment* enters the frame—that special kind of envy

59. Ibid., pp. 108–9.

60. Ibid., p. 108.

61. Scheler, *Ressentiment*, p. 67.

62. Wurmser, *The Superego as Herald of Resentment*, pp. 387, 397.

concerned with value delusions. It may well be that their proposed reimagining of values stands on solid ground—but the ongoing confusion over what exactly decolonization entails, suggests the presence of a 'way of thinking which attributes creative power to mere negation'.[61] To be clear, talk of decolonizing consciousness has been a staple of the academic circuit for more than half a century—and it is the lack of resolution that turns Fallist politics into a legitimate object of *ressentiment* analysis.

It is my contention that several Fallist motifs bind the student movement to *ressentiment* politics. The first involves the *ressentiment* subject's adoption of what Léon Wurmser calls the position of 'innocent victim'.[62] Regardless of their actual behaviour— and this is a matter of public record—student activists considered themselves beyond reproach and therefore entirely free of guilt, there being (in Kleinian terms) no transition

63. Ibid., p. 397.

64. Ibid., p. 396.

65. Scheler, *Ressentiment*, p. 69.

66. Hoggett, 'Ressentiment and grievance'. See citation of Steiner (1993) on pp. 396–397.

67. Wahbie Long, 'Decolonizing Higher Education: Postcolonial Theory and the Invisible Hand of Student Politics', *New Agenda*, 69 (2018), pp. 20–25.

to depressive functioning. A second point of convergence—described again by Wurmser—is the moral absolutism of the *ressentiment* universe, which manifests itself at the individual level as an 'anal-sadomasochistic superego operating in absolute polarities'.[63] For those of us who followed the university protests, the twin tropes of white privilege and black pain were seared into our consciousness, leaving little room for the contemplation of moral and political ambiguities. The complexity of our political situation was whittled down to the simple moral binary of 'with us or against us'. And third, the classic sign of the *ressentiment* mood is the displacement of a suppressed impulse for revenge onto substitute objects.[64] Scheler describes how *ressentiment*—through repression—involves the disconnection of the person in question from 'the original object of an emotion' with the result that the person 'does not know "of what" he [or she] is afraid

or incapable'.[65] In this regard, as much as elite university culture can leave black students struggling with feelings of alienation, it is not the primary locus of the problem. My reading is that Fallist rage originates in prior humiliations—misrecognitions—that are raced, classed, and gendered in complex ways. Shame, after all, is hardwired into the chronicity of everyday and structural violence: unable to exact revenge, the original trauma that is structural violence is forgotten—but the sense of injury remains. It is picked at compulsively, eventually exploding without warning onto unwitting secondary targets. And as John Steiner points out in his work on grievance, the victim position is not easily relinquished:[66] it is a source of satisfaction that is narcissistically invested, hence the seeming self-aggrandizement of Fallist supporters.

What remains to be examined, then, is the decisive matter of values. In my own writings, I have described the term 'decolonization' as an 'empty signifier':[67] notice the oddity, for example, of intellectuals stressing the importance of 'decolonizing' higher education *before* they commence discussions on what it actually means. Indeed—as the post-Marxist Ernesto Laclau points out—it is *because* it lacks any definite meaning that the

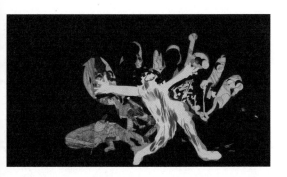

decolonization discourse can frame the political landscape—at least symbolically—in compelling ways.[68] In a post-truth world that has presided over the relativization of all knowledge claims, decolonization discourse is not required to justify itself; its seat at the high table of epistemology is reserved. Yet it is a highly suspect form of politics because it often looks for problems in the wrong places. To begin with, proponents of decolonization almost never acknowledge one basic fact—that most poor and working-class students have suffered the indignity of being miseducated for twelve years of their lives. South Africa's schooling system ranks consistently among the worst in the world and by the time these students enter elite universities, they are hopelessly underprepared for the academic life and struggle to cope with the unrelenting institutional demands. But instead of acknowledging these difficulties as areas for personal development, like Aesop's fox they conclude that the grapes must be sour *because* they are unreachable. The problem is not the collective injustice they suffered in our dysfunctional schools—rather, it becomes the university system and the Enlightenment values it espouses. It does not matter that no one knows

68. Ernesto Laclau, *On Populist Reason* (London: Verso, 2005).

69. Vivek Chibber, *Social Determinants of Psychological Suffering (with Reference to Marx's Theory of Alienation).* Seminar delivered at Child Guidance Clinic, University of Cape Town, 8 August 2017.

what decolonization means—the university must be decolonized regardless—and so it comes to pass that what Vivek Chibber calls 'an orgy of bullshit'[69] gets treated deferentially as *bona fide* scholarship.

It is no accident that—in the post-apartheid years—there has never been a Fallist movement in our township schools. Everyone receives the same inferior education and—because of Cape Town's enduring apartheid-style geography—there is scant awareness of the first-rate education learners in the leafy Southern Suburbs are receiving. But when these school-leavers enter elite universities, the inevitable social comparisons begin. A feeling of relative deprivation emerges as the political ideal of equality collides with the social reality of inequality. Poor and working-class students observe the ease with which their more privileged counterparts appear to negotiate university spaces. Envious resentment flares up among those students most alienated from the social order. What

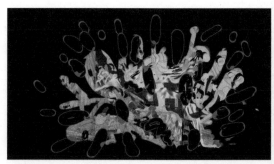

70. See Scheler, *Ressentiment*, p. 66; also Coser, 'Max Scheler', p. 30.

71. Coser, 'Max Scheler', pp. 28–30.

72. Scheler, *Ressentiment*, p. 60.

73. Long, *Decolonizing Higher Education*, p. 23.

74. Fukuyama, *Identity*; see also Vivek Chibber, 'Rescuing Class from the Cultural Turn', *Catalyst* 1, no. 1 (2017), pp. 27–56.

are they to do? Because they desire a middle-class existence—why else would anyone go to university?—they cannot draw on the traditional values of the working class.[70] Frustrated and without counter-values of their own, they can only attack the existing institutional order, despising it in public yet desiring it in secret.[71] They have forgotten the original crime—their own miseducation—and vent their anger at the university authorities instead. At this point, the politics of decolonization becomes the politics of displacement. It does not stand on its own ground, being fundamentally a *reaction* against the Enlightenment tradition. It is a resounding 'No!' to the affirmations of the academic establishment. Yet its proponents are also tortured by their own *ressentiment*—because the values they abhor consciously are the same values their educational aspirations demand that they embrace. On this point it is worth quoting Scheler once more:

[A] man [sic] who 'slanders' the unattainable values which oppress him is by no means completely unaware of their positive character … the positive values are still felt as such, but they are *overcast* by the false values and can shine through only dimly. The ressentiment experience is always characterized by this 'transparent' presence of the true and objective values behind the illusory ones—by that obscure awareness that one lives in a *sham world* which one is unable to penetrate.[72]

One would be mistaken in assuming that the future of South Africa depends entirely on the condition of the poor and working classes. (I, for one, have made that assumption before.[73]) To prove the point, one need only ask oneself why our country has not yet descended into civil war. The short answer is that the exploited classes do not have the wherewithal to organize themselves into a viable force—and that verdict has been reached on both the political left and right.[74] That is why the influence of *middle-class ressentiment* should not be underestimated. There is of course a substantial gap between the ivory tower and the street—but it is equally true that what happens

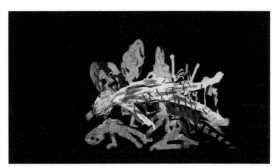

on university campuses filters into public spaces. I mention this because research conducted in the middle of the twentieth century showed how followers of fascist movements were most likely to come from the lower strata of the middle classes who—because their strivings for self-improvement were continuously blocked—were most susceptible to developing feelings of *ressentiment*.[75] At present, colleagues around the country inform me of the increasingly fascist tenor of campus politics: they describe the suppression of dissent, rampant opportunism, and ideological dishonesty. We see the same in national politics as quasi-fascist movements swim ever closer to the political mainstream. With the degree of cooperation between the two spheres increasing all the time—and with social inequality showing few signs of abating—it is only a matter of time before impotent rage—*ressentiment*—gets channelled into the creation of anti-democratic political movements.

Impasse
In the mid-1950s, the French psychoanalyst, Octave Mannoni, published what would become his most famous work, *Prospero and Caliban*. In his attempt to understand the psychological workings of

75. Coser, 'Max Scheler', p. 31.

76. Bulhan, *Frantz Fanon and the Psychology of Oppression*, pp. 107–113.

colonialism, Mannoni assigned a dependency complex to the colonized, which he believed expressed itself via a reaction formation in the shape of a pathological desire for freedom. It is a highly contentious argument that I cannot take up now. Instead, I want to focus on two of Mannoni's observations on the psychology of the colonizer.[76] First, Mannoni reasoned that the cultural and technological achievements of Europe—powered by enterprise, ingenuity and an urge to dominate—were in fact the products of a defensive maneuver against an underlying inferiority complex. Second, he suggested that the need to rule in faraway lands stemmed from a paradoxical hatred of humankind. Pouring out of Europe—spurred on by their own misanthropy—the colonizers set out in search of worlds

77. Octave Mannoni, *Prospero and Caliban: The Psychology of Colonization*, trans. P. Powesland (London: Methuen, 1956), p. 101.

78. Ibid., p. 117.

79. Bulhan, *Frantz Fanon and the Psychology of Oppression*, p. 116.

80. Alexandre Kojève, *Introduction to the Reading of Hegel: Lectures on the Phenomenology of Spirit*, trans. J.H. Nichols, Jr. (Ithaca: Cornell University Press, 1947/1980), p. 19.

81. G. Straker, 'Race for Cover: Castrated Whiteness, Perverse Consequences', *Psychoanalytic Dialogues*, 14, no. 4 (2004), pp. 405–22.

82. Melanie Suchet, 'Unraveling Whiteness', in *Relational Psychoanalysis: Expansion of Theory*, Vol. 4, ed. L. Aron and A. Harris, pp. 199–220 (New York: Routledge, 2012).

83. Ibid., p. 211, emphasis added.

of the colonial project was at stake—in Mannoni's words,

> we are perfectly happy if we can project the fantasies of our own unconscious onto the outside world, but if we suddenly find that these creatures are not pure projections but real beings with claims to liberty, we consider it outrageous.[78]

they fantasized would bear no trace of a human presence. High on 'the lure of a world without men',[77] it was easy to convince themselves that they had 'discovered' America and Australia and southern Africa—in spite of the presence of the local populations—because the locals did not qualify as fully human. Rather, the colonizers would project their own forbidden impulses onto the subhuman creatures they encountered. Obsessed especially with the sexual rapacity of the natives and the clear and present danger to their own delicate women, the savages had to be infantilized, paternalized, or subdued by force—and any attempt by the colonized to declare their own humanity was to be suppressed by all means necessary. This was no simple matter of economic or strategic interest—the psychological equilibrium

As the Fanonian scholar Hussein Bulhan explains, colonizers are tragic figures. On the one hand, they need the colonized to remain in their place, to serve as the repository of their projections, a fate that no human being will tolerate indefinitely. On the other—since the colonial relationship is a recapitulation of the master-slave dialectic[79]—the colonizer never feels recognized as human because the act of recognition is made by a slave and is therefore worthless. It is this hapless situation that constitutes what Kojève calls the 'existential impasse' of the master[80]—a situation that I believe may apply to many white South Africans today.

Progressive white psychoanalysts including Gillian Straker[81] and Melanie Suchet[82] have written courageously about their racial melancholia as 'the *unwilling* beneficiaries of Whiteness'.[83]

But we neglect at our peril those whites whose racial melancholia is all about a *'refusal* to relinquish what has been lost'.[84] As Suchet admits in the postscript to her chapter, 'Unraveling Whiteness', this refusal involves *most* white South Africans. Indeed, the end of apartheid has not led to significant changes in the distribution of material resources—but the passage of time does appear to have exposed the fragility of whiteness. Uncertain of their place in South African life, many whites have withdrawn from public spaces into fortified enclaves[85]—'their gated communities with high walls, electrified fences, closed-circuit television and private [armies]'.[86] The steady erosion of whiteness has produced a sense of loss and confusion: as per Suchet's analysis, what was once a narcissistic veneer has been replaced by a melancholic structure. No longer do black people submit to the white subject's fantasy: they are exiting the dialectic *en masse*, leaving the master without a *raison d'être*. Disoriented, it is as though white South Africans were asking their black counterparts—and I quote Suchet again—'If you are no longer that to me, then who am I to myself?'[87] But rather than step into the void between whiteness and blackness, many white people have simply

84. Ibid., p. 217, emphasis added.

85. Charlotte Lemanski, 'A New Apartheid? The Spatial Implications of Fear of Crime in Cape Town, South Africa', *Environment and Urbanization* 16, no. 2 (2004), pp. 101–111.

86. Long, 'Essence or Experience?', p. 308.

87. Suchet, 'Unraveling Whiteness', p. 217.

88. Ibid., p. 205.

89. Straker, 'Race for Cover', p. 412.

90. Slavoj Žižek, *Violence: Six Sideways Reflections* (New York: Picador, 2008), p. 53.

91. Rupert Woodfin and Oscar Zarate, *Introducing Marxism: A Graphic Guide* (Royston, UK: Icon Books, 2004), p. 65.

battened down the hatches, retreating still further into their whiteness: they live (barely) in an existential impasse, refusing to recognize black people and, being unable to resolve their grief, they cling stubbornly to their lost object—just as Freud's melancholics once did.[88] In an evident case of disavowal, they know what is happening yet still they believe,[89] or, as Slavoj Žižek puts it, 'I know, but I don't want to know that I know, so I don't know'.[90]

Disavowal is made possible through its connection with fetishism. Marx described the commodity fetish as the expropriation of workers' labour power, which then reappears magically in the products of their labour.[91] The commodity comes to

92. Straker, 'Race for Cover',
pp. 413–414.

93. Mitchell, 'You've Got to
Suffer If You Want to Sing
the Blues: Psychoanalytic
Reflections on Guilt and Self-
pity', *Psychoanalytic Dialogues*
10, no. 5 (2000), pp. 713–733.
See p. 731.

94. N. Altman, 'Whiteness
Uncovered: Commentary on
papers by Melanie Suchet and
Gillian Straker', *Psychoanalytic
Dialogues*, 14, no. 4 (2004), pp.
439–446, here p. 442.

95. Suchet, 'Unraveling
Whiteness', p. 212.

96. Straker, 'Race for Cover',
pp. 407, 420.

97. Deborah Posel, 'Races to
Consume: Revisiting South
Africa's History of Race,
Consumption and the Struggle
for Freedom', *Ethnic and
Racial Studies* 33, no. 2 (2010),
pp. 157–175, here p. 167.

98. Mitchell, 'You've Got to
Suffer If You Want to Sing the
Blues'; Adrienne Harris, 'The
House of Difference, or White
Silence', *Studies in Gender and
Sexuality* 13, no. 3 (2012), pp.
197–216, here p. 204.

99. Harris, 'The House of
Difference, or White Silence',
p. 207.

100. Ibid.

represent what has been lost: the target of powerful identifications, it is converted readily into a fetish. Following Straker's line of argument, one may reason that white South Africans manage their experience of lack and loss through fetishism, their castrated whiteness affirmed and negated simultaneously.[92] Locked away in their gated communities—a symbol of what Stephen Mitchell has called an 'internal protection racket'[93]— commodities overcome them in splendid isolation,[94] this their defense againt the brittleness of whiteness.[95] Perversion has entered the scene, the anxiety generated by lack papered over by the fetish.[96]

Deborah Posel notes how '[r]ace is always a relational construct'[97]—the meaning of whiteness both implies and depends on the meaning of blackness—but with black people refusing to endorse the historical terms of reference, white people find themselves in psychic freefall, cut loose from what was once subjective *and* objective truth. Too many deny their moral culpability, their defensiveness typical of paranoid-schizoid guiltiness rather than depressive guilt.[98] Reflecting on this inability to mourn, Adrienne Harris describes a gap in the white psyche that functions as 'an imploding star, refusing signification', where not only trauma but also destructiveness has been bleached out.[99] All the while, the loss of the white ideal is disavowed through the commodity fetish with its stockpiling of economic power, no matter the attendant psychosocial damage.[100]

Strictly speaking, Kojève's 'existential impasse' refers to the master's realization that he has not been intersubjectively confirmed: he turns the Other into his slave in order to be recognized yet the slave by definition is not worthy of recognizing him. The situation I am describing, however, is one in which it is black people who see through the rules of engagement—although the outcome for white people as putative masters

is still the same. Kojève explains how the master realizes that he is on the 'wrong track [yet he] has no desire to "overcome" ... himself as master... he cannot be transformed, educated... Mastery is the supreme given value for him, beyond which he cannot go'.[101] Without the prospect of redemption, the master can only continue as before. Kojève again:

> The Master ... does not work, [he] produces nothing stable outside of himself. He merely destroys the products of the Slave's work [by consuming them]. Thus his enjoyment and his satisfaction remain purely subjective: they are of interest only to him and therefore can be recognized only by him; they have no 'truth', no objective reality revealed to all. Accordingly, this 'consumption', this idle enjoyment of the Master's, which results from the 'immediate' satisfaction of desire, can at the most procure some pleasure for man; it can never give him complete and definitive satisfaction.[102]

Whereas the style of the black middle class is to consume their goods in plain sight,[103] white consumers do so seemingly in private. As far as I can

101. Kojève, *Introduction to the Reading of Hegel*, pp. 19, 21–22.

102. Ibid., p. 24.

103. Ronelle Burger et al., 'Understanding Consumption Patterns of the Established and Emerging South African Black Middle Class', *Development Southern Africa* 32, no. 1 (2015), pp. 41–56.

104. Raewynn W. Connell, *Southern Theory: The Global Dynamics of Knowledge in Social Science* (Cambridge, UK: Polity Press, 2007), p. 216.

tell, this is not because white people do not need to signal their status; it is rather the case that white consumption is an exercise submerged in guiltiness. The difference in consumption habits may explain why we still know rather little about the goings-on in the homes of the white elite; indeed, it is only by 'studying up' that the workings of the master-slave dialectic can be articulated in full.[104] On the basis of this analysis, however, it would appear that, in the drawing rooms of private urban enclaves, it is impasse, inwardness and joylessness that prevail, the hallmarks of whiteness in post-apartheid South Africa.

Hope
In tracing the trajectories of shame, envy and impasse in our national life, I have attempted to place Hegel's master-slave dialectic front and centre. But one also needs to situate the question of equality in historical

105. Walter Scheidel, *The Great Leveler: Violence and the History of Inequality from the Stone Age to the Twenty-first Century* (Princeton: Princeton University Press, 2017).

106. Ibid.

context: never mind South Africa, it is a sobering fact that the history of our *species* is a history of masters and slaves. In his account of social organization from the Stone Age to the present, Walter Scheidel contends that a combination of domesticated food production, sedentism, state formation and hereditary property rights ensured that material inequality became a central feature of human coexistence.[105] A fundamental part of the civilizing process, in other words, is inequality itself. But history is not without surprises. What Scheidel calls the *Four Horsemen of Leveling* is proof that unequal societies can be leveled—in exchange for a monumental loss of life. *Mass mobilization warfare* is one of those horsemen involving the kind of killing contract that more or less seeps into every segment of society. The two world wars are fitting examples where industrial-scale warfare, aggressive taxation, rising costs of living, state involvement in the economy, and trade disruptions ravaged the wealth of the rich, leading to unionization and the creation of welfare states that would level inequality on a scale almost unparalleled in human history. *Transformative revolution* is another notable leveler. Communist takeovers—exemplified by expropriation, redistribution, and collectivization—succeeded in challenging inequality in extraordinary ways, rivaling even the world wars for number of fatalities and human suffering in general. *State failure* is the third horseman: when states fall apart, the rich simply have more to lose so the playing fields get evened out. And finally, there are *lethal pandemics*: when sufficient numbers of people die, the balance between capital and labour can shift so dramatically that one can be left with Black Death-type situations where the workers make merry on meat and beer while the nobles run around trying to maintain appearances.

Acts of God aside, Scheidel is clear that *exemplary violence alone* has been shown to address inequality in genuine ways—not democracy, not macroeconomic crises, not modern economic development, not even radical policy reforms.[106] Fanon may well have intuited this when

Just to be sure they bashed her head with a stone.

she was 8 years old

he declared that 'decolonization is always a violent phenomenon'.[107] Naturally, the irony of seeking to end structural and symbolic violence with *revolutionary* violence is not lost on anyone; indeed, the wellsprings of life-giving hope may have to be sought elsewhere. But the basic point is this: the cultivation of hope in the absence of actual material prospects amounts to little more than another cheap opiate for the masses. Real hope cannot exist within a matrix of shame, envy and impasse when the material base of our disfigured national psyche remains locked in place. As for the observable correlates of everyday violence, *ressentiment*-driven value delusions and alienated consumptiveness, these should remind us that nothing less than our shared humanity is at stake.

The only way to dissolve the master-slave dialectic is to resolve the problem of unreciprocated recognition in which the master insists on remaining the master. Fanon envisioned a particular outcome to the deadlock but it is not a solution that builds nations. As psychologists, we tend to treat misrecognition as a 'psychical deformation'; philosophers regard it as a matter of 'ethical self-realization'.[108] Neither of these positions will suffice. Following Nancy

107. Fanon, *The Wretched of the Earth*, p. 27.

108. Fraser, *Redistribution or Recognition?*, p. 29.

109. Ibid., original emphasis.

110. Martha Nussbaum, *Sex and Social Justice* (New York: Oxford University Press, 1999).

Fraser, I want to reframe the question of misrecognition as a question of *justice*—because misrecognition involves 'an institutionalized relation of *subordination*',[109] a relation that prevents South Africans from participating as peers in a dignified social life.

But what makes for a life of dignity, what makes a life incontrovertibly human? One can hardly do better than Martha Nussbaum's catalogue of ten central human capabilities.[110] This is not the occasion to repeat the entire list, so allow me to quote only those of her reflections that are of immediate relevance. For Nussbaum, being human means

> Being able to move freely from place to place... Being able to use the senses; being able to imagine, to think, and to reason and to do these things in a 'truly human' way, a way informed and cultivated by an adequate education... Being able to form a conception of the good and

111. Ibid., pp. 41–2.

112. Long, 'Essence or Experience?', p. 308.

to engage in critical reflection about the planning of one's own life… Being able to live for and in relation to others, to recognize and show concern for other human beings, to engage in various forms of social interaction; being able to imagine the situation of another and to have compassion for that situation; having the capability for both justice and friendship… Having the social bases of self-respect and nonhumiliation; being able to be treated as a dignified being whose worth is equal to that of others… being able to participate effectively in political choices that govern one's life… being able to hold property… being able to work as a human being, exercising practical reason and entering into meaningful relationships of mutual recognition with other workers.[111]

Anything less and the life under consideration is no longer a human life.

Notice Nussbaum's emphasis on *material* space: the freedom to move from one place to another, the reality of owning property. These are among the attributes that make us human. For the millions of disenfranchised South Africans, therefore, the question of landlessness is not only of practical importance: it is an existential question. To own land is to own oneself, to live with confidence in the world, to build communities of feeling, to pursue questions of meaning rather than survival, to have the sense that one is ontologically real.[112] To deny a people their land, therefore, is to deny them their humanity. Ominously, Scheidel makes the point that land reform—when accompanied by violence or the threat of violence—is an effective strategy for levelling inequality. Why is violence or the threat of it effective? Because no one gives up anything worthwhile without a struggle. One can only hope that it does not come to that, that the power elite in this country will recognize that the interests of the dispossessed are the interests of us all.

But Nussbaum also discusses *psychological* capacities in her account of what it is to be human. We should not make the error, therefore, of imagining that the psychological is trivial in contexts of massive material deprivation. The land question is

#malawinotebooks
2 May 2020
Thinking of Asifa

critical—and its resolution will go some way towards restoring dignity to the lives of South Africans—but we must not underestimate the *political* relevance of our ability for recognizing and validating the mental states of others. Treat others as you wish to be treated and do not treat others in a manner that you do not wish to be treated: this is the so-called 'Golden Rule' that underpins almost every religious, cultural and ethical system known to humankind. Yet one cannot realize this principle without a capacity for empathy—and that is what marks us out as psychotherapists. We are experts at holding minds in mind— at perspective-taking—a prerequisite for ethical living. But it is just as true that empathic sensitivity becomes damaging when it is oblivious to the political struggles of ordinary people. That is why critical theory matters, why sociology matters, why philosophy matters, why history matters, why economics matters. The parent discipline we call psychology is a discipline of the *status quo*:[113] progressive practice requires of us a preparedness to venture outside our home discipline. The splitting of the psychological from the social domain has made it difficult for psychologists to have any kind of moral voice in the struggles of the everyday. On the other hand, the tendency among many activists to dismiss psychology as false consciousness is premature to say the least. The bottom line is that personal change and social transformation are inseparable: as much as we need programmes for

113. Isaac Prilleltensky, 'Psychology and the Status Quo', *American Psychologist* 44, no. 5 (1989), pp. 795–802.

social improvement, we also need to remember that the small things still matter. That is just one of the things we as psychotherapists do: we nurture hope—that most fragile of cargoes— with the realization that what each of us does in our lives on a moment-to-moment basis will ripple through the ages.

HUMAN CAPABILITIES

SHAME! and Masculinity

INA VAN ZYL

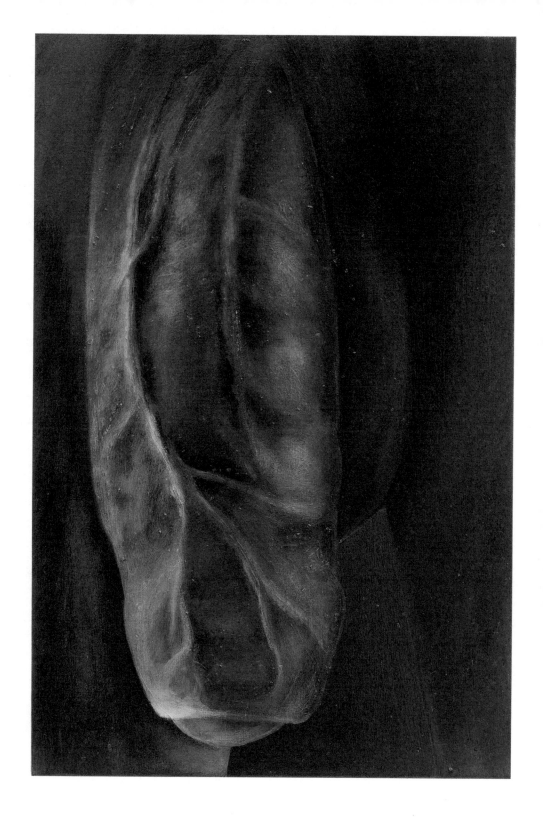

Lul, 2010
oil on linen, 60 x 40 cm

SHAME! and Masculinity

Skaamrosie Teen Skemer, 2009
oil on linen, 50 x 40 cm

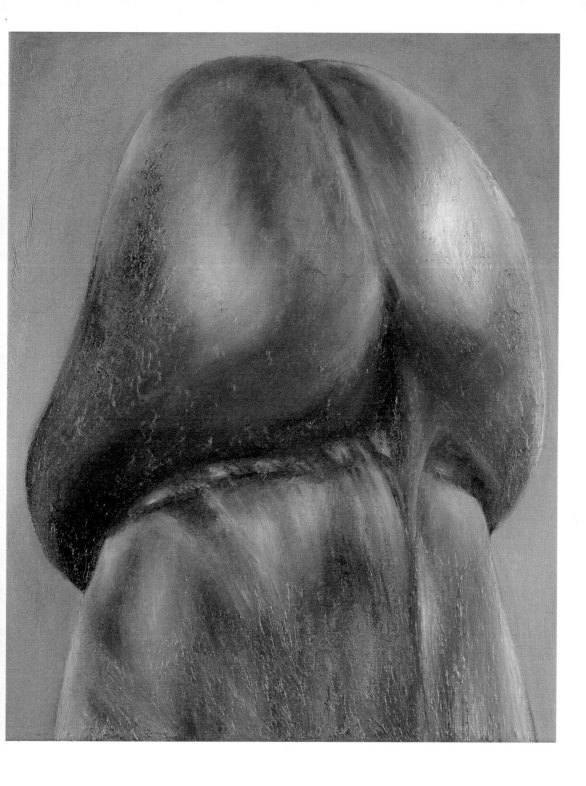

Ina van Zyl

Circumcised, 2006
oil on linen, 55 x 45 cm

SHAME! and Masculinity

Montagne, 2010
oil on linen, 60 x 50 cm

Ina van Zyl

Skaamrosie, 2007
oil on linen, 50 x 40 cm

Dogtertjie, 2010
oil on linen, 60 x 40 cm

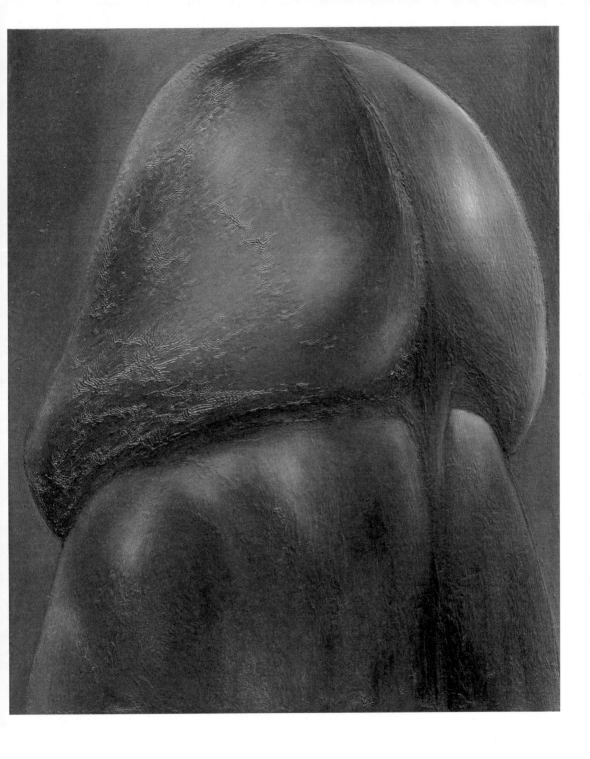

Ina van Zyl

Dick By Dawn, 2009
oil on linen, 60 x 50 cm

HANS HOVY

Pure Love, 2008/2010/2013
white soapstone, pink soapstone, 16.1 x 22.9 x 19.6 cm

SHAME! and Masculinity

Two Proud Man, 2007/2018/2019
wood, glass, 22.7 x 73.7 x 36.8 cm

Hans Hovy

Small Sodom, 2007/2008/2013/2020
white alabaster, pink soapstone,
33.4 x 32.6 x 29.2 cm

Dream, 2009/2013
translucent alabaster, pink soapstone,
34.5 x 45 x 41.8 cm

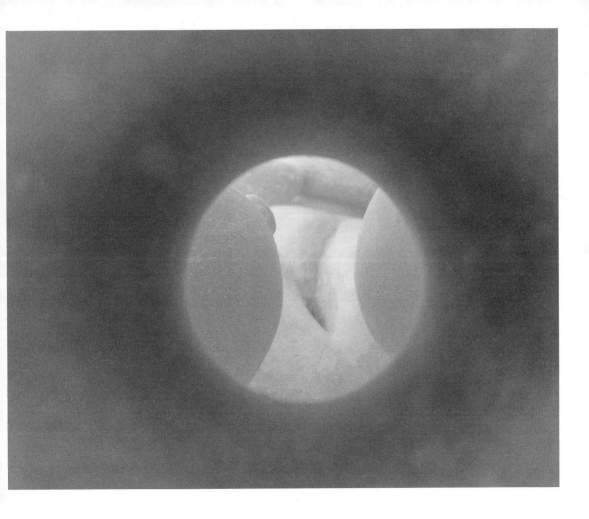

Dreaming of a Beautiful World (detail of inside),
2012/2013/2020
translucent alabaster, pink soapstone, 21 x 30.9 x 24 cm

Hans Hovy

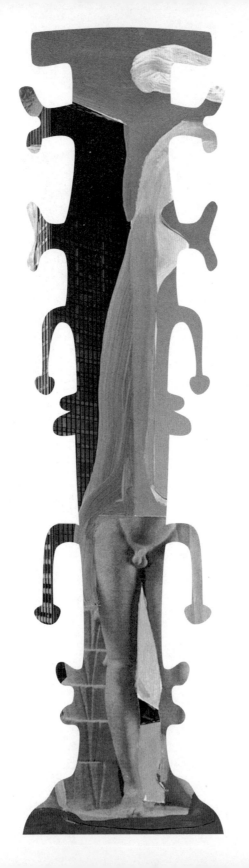

H401

Shame! and Masculinitiy is part of a public programme with an exhibition, performance, soundscape, workshops and lectures, initiated and implemented by the Amsterdam-based foundation **H401**. Through artistic research and together with its audience, it explores the role of shame in relation to power within sexuality and more specifically the relationship between male sexuality and male authority. The programme focuses on the collusions and collisions of shame and male sexuality in the history of the visual arts and in socio-cultural relationships and behaviour and invites all readers to participate in the conversation we wish to fuel and facilitate.

H401's interest in the human condition is based on the rich and complex history of its house at Herengracht 401 in Amsterdam, where lives have been saved and other lives disrupted, people have been inspired and others damaged (for more context see h401.org/about/). Its history has motivated us to explore ambiguous concepts such as *vulnerability for group fanaticism* (2011), *freedom* (2012), *friendship* (2013), *participation in the arts* (2014), *collective and cultural memory and the construction of identity* (2015), *the female perspective* (2017). Under the motto: *Memory Machine—We Are What We Remember,* **H401** developed numerous artistic research activities throughout the last decade. It led to international collaborative projects with universities, civil society, and cultural organizations from Europe and South America, that deal with traumatic pasts. Trauma as a direct consequence of power abuse is often linked to the notion of masculinity. Reason enough for **H401** to creatively explore the boundaries of this cultural construct and initiate co-operations that may contribute to a better awareness and understanding of the role cultural conventions play in human nature.

Michael Defuster, Lars Ebert, Frans Damman – H401

www.H401.org
mail@H401.org

BIOGRAPHIES

Ernst van Alphen (b. 1958) is a cultural analyst employed by the University of Leiden. Book publications include *Failed Images: Photography and its Counter-Practices* (Valiz, 2018); *Staging the Archive: Art and Photography in the Age of New Media* (Reaktion Books, 2014); *Art in Mind: How Contemporary Images Shape Thought* (University of Chicago Press, 2005), *Caught by History: Holocaust Effects in Art, Literature, and Theory* (Stanford University Press, 1997); *Francis Bacon and the Loss of Self* (Harvard University Press, 1993). Van Alphen lives and works in Amsterdam and Paris.

Lorenzo Benadusi (b. 1973) is professor of Contemporary History and History of European Culture at Roma Tre University. He served as postdoctoral fellow in the International Humanities Program at Brown University, Providence, RI. His work analyzes the history of masculinity and homosexuality from the unification of Italy to the Fascist period. Recent books include *Respectability and Violence: Military Values, Masculine Honor, and Italy's Road to Mass Death* (University of Wisconsin Press, forthcoming); *Homosexuality in Italian Literature, Society, and Culture, 1789–1919* (co-edited with Paolo L. Bernardini, Elisa Bianco, Paola Guazzo, Cambridge Scholars Publishing, 2017); *George L. Mosse's Italy: Interpretation, Reception, and Intellectual Heritage* (co-edit with Giorgio Caravale, Palgrave Macmillan, 2014); *The Enemy of the New Man: Homosexuality in Fascist Italy* (University of Wisconsin Press, 2012). Benadusi lives and works in Rome.

Jeannette Christensen (b. 1958) artist, studied at the West Coast Academy of Art (Vestlandets kunstakademi), Bergen, Norway and the Ecole nationale supérieure des Beaux-Arts, Paris. She is currently professor of Contemporary Art at the National Academy of Fine Art, Oslo, since 2010. Christensen works with installations, sculpture, and photography. Recent exhibitions: 'Interruptions', KODE 3, Bergen, 2020; 'Woman Interrupted', Kunstplass Contemporary Art, Oslo, 2017. Recent publication: Mieke Bal with Jeannette Christensen, 'An Aesthetic of Interruption: Stagnation and Acceleration', *ASAP/Journal* 4.1 (January 2019). Christensen lives and works in Oslo.

Marlene Dumas (b. 1953) is an artist with a BA in Fine Arts from the University of Cape Town (1972–1975). In 1976 she came to the Netherlands and attended Ateliers '63 in Haarlem (1976–1978). She is well known for her interest in the relation between image and text. Her paintings and drawings, often devoted to depictions of the human form, are typically culled from a vast archive of images collected by the artist. Recent exhibitions: 'Double Takes', Zeno X, Antwerp, 2020; 'Moonrise: Marlene Dumas & Edvard Munch', Munchmuseet, Oslo, 2018–2019; 'Myths & Mortals', David Zwirner, New York, 2018; 'The Image as Burden', Stedelijk Museum Amsterdam, 2014–2015; 'Measuring Your Own Grave', Museum of Modern Art, New York, 2008–2009. Dumas lives and works in Amsterdam.

Adeola Enigbokan

is an artist and urbanist based in Mexico City. Her research practice is informed by theory and methods from environmental psychology, anthropology and historical studies. She conducts research on urban experience with architects, designers, educators and other social researchers in neighbourhoods of New York, Tel Aviv, Moscow, Saint Petersburg, Beijing, Mexico City and Amsterdam. She holds an MPhil in Anthropology and Historical Studies from The New School for Social Research, and a PhD in Environmental Psychology from the City University of New York, based on her doctoral dissertation, *Archiving the City: A Guide to the Art of Urban Interventions*.

Tijs Goldschmidt

(b. 1953) is a behavioural biologist and essayist. His publications include the book *Darwin's Dreampond* (MIT Press, 1996) and the collections of essays *Wolven op het ruiterpad: Over mensen en andere roedeldieren* and *Vis in bad* (Athenaeum, 2020 and 2014). In April 2019, a selection of his letters was published: *Onvoldoende liefdesbrieven*. He holds an advisory position at the Rijksakademie van beeldende kunsten in Amsterdam and is a 'dormant' guest writer at Artis Library.

Arnoud Holleman

(b. 1964) is an artist, filmmaker, and writer, who studied at the Royal Academy of Art in The Hague and the Rijksakademie van beeldende kunsten in Amsterdam. His extraordinarily diverse output is thematically connected by a strong concern with the life and significance of images. He has made drama and documentaries for television, worked in theatre, and was co-editor of *RE-Magazine*. He had solo exhibitions in the Frans Hals Museum Haarlem, Van Abbemuseum Eindhoven and Stedelijk Museum Bureau Amsterdam. He also participated in numerous group shows, both in the Netherlands and abroad, including the Gwangju Biennale of 2010. Currently, Holleman teaches at the Sandberg Instituut in Amsterdam. He lives and works in Monnickendam.

Hans Hovy

(b. 1953), was a participant at the institute De Ateliers, then in Haarlem, from 1981–1983, after earning a postgraduate teaching diploma at the Amsterdam Academie voor Beeldende Vorming. His works include outdoor commissions, sculptures, glass and ceramic objects, jewelry, drawings, prints, drinking glasses, carpets, and walking sticks. Hovy lives and works in Amsterdam, and is represented there by Galerie

Onrust and Galerie Rob Koudijs, and in Rotterdam by Galerie Christian Ouwens. Solo exhibitions at Galerie Onrust include 'King of Sculpture', 2019; 'Glassobs', 2017; 'Sculptissimo', 2014; and 'Sculptullery' at Galerie Rob Koudijs, 2010. In 2014–2015 the Gemeentemuseum (now Kunstmuseum) Den Haag, The Hague, mounted a solo show, 'Sculptissimo'.

Natasja Kensmil (b. 1973) studied
at Rietveld Academie and De Ateliers. She uses quotes from history in her work to highlight the relationship between the present and the past. Solo exhibitions: 'Monument of Regents', Amsterdam Museum/Hermitage Amsterdam, 2020; 'In the light of time' (with Nicoline Timmer) andriesse eyck gallery, Amsterdam, 2018; 'Crying Light', Royal Hibernian Academy, Dublin, 2013. Group exhibitions: 'In the Presence of Absence', Stedelijk Museum Amsterdam, 2020. 'No Man's Land: Women Artists from the Rubell Family Collection', National Museum of Women in the Arts, Washington, 2016. Publication: *Hellmouth* (Andriesse Eyck Publications, 2016) with texts by Hans den Hartog Jager and Diana Franssen. Kensmil lives and works in Amsterdam.

Wahbie Long (b. 1980) is a
clinical psychologist who studied at the University of Cape Town and Stellenbosch University, South Africa. He is an associate professor in the Department of Psychology at the University of Cape Town,

and has held research fellowships at Durham and Harvard. His current research explores the application of psychoanalytic theory to social and political life. Widely published in periodicals such as *History of Psychology, Journal of Theoretical and Philosophical Psychology*, and *New Ideas in Psychology*, he is the author of *A History of 'Relevance' in Psychology* (Palgrave, 2016). Long lives and works in Cape Town.

Nalini Malani (b. 1946) in Karachi
(Undivided India) studied at the Sir JJ School of Art in Mumbai. In order to reach a wider audience, and as a protest against the rise of orthodox elements in politics, since the late 1980s she has been creating immersive painting installations, theatre, ephemeral wall drawings, erasure performances, and her signature video/shadow plays. Recent solo museum exhibitions include 'You Don't Hear Me', Joan Miró Foundation, Barcelona, 2020; 'The Rebellion of the Dead: Retrospective 1969–2018, Part II', Castello di Rivoli—Contemporary Art Museum, Turin, 2018; 'The Rebellion of the Dead: Retrospective 1969–2018, Part I', Centre Pompidou, Paris, 2017. Malani lives and works in Mumbai.

Maaike Meijer (b. 1949) is an
emeritus professor of Gender Studies at Maastricht University, now active as an independent journalist and academic writer. She has published on Dutch literature and culture, on poetry, songs and other forms of popular

culture, on feminism, gender theory, and the ethics of representation. Recent publications include biographies of Dutch women-poets: *Hemelse mevrouw Frederike: Biografie van F. Harmsen van Beek 1927–2009* (De Bezige Bij, 2018) and *M. Vasalis* (Van Oorschot, 2011). She is currently working on a study of shifting cultural representations of masculinity. Meijer lives and works in Amsterdam.

Philip Miller (b. 1964) is a
South African composer and sound artist. His starting point is often to draw from sonic material from public and personal archives, which he then digitally processes and collages. He works across different musical genres and media leading him to establish significant collaborations including his long-time collaborator, South African artist William Kentridge. He has been the recipient of fellowships and residencies including The Rockefeller Foundation Bellagio Center, Civitella Ranieri Foundation, Yaddo, and the Archive & Public Culture (APC) Initiative at the University of Cape Town.

Andrea Pető (b. 1964) is a historian
and a professor at the Department of Gender Studies at Central European University, Budapest, and a Doctor of Science of the Hungarian Academy of Sciences. Her works on gender, politics, Holocaust, and war have been translated into 23 languages. In 2018 she was awarded the 2018 All European Academies (ALLEA)

Madame de Staël Prize for Cultural Values. Recent publications include *The Women of the Arrow Cross Party: Invisible Hungarian Perpetrators in the Second World War* (Palgrave Macmillan, 2020). Pető lives in Budapest and in Vienna.

Artur Żmijewski (b. 1966) is an
artist. He studied at Warsaw Academy of Fine Arts from 1990–1995; focused as an artist on film, photography, collages and sculptures; curator of the 7th Berlin Biennale in 2012; co-editor of *Forget Fear*, the book accompanying the 7th Berlin Biennale. Żmijewski participated in the 2007 and 2017 editions of documenta. He had an exhibition in the Polish Pavilion during the Venice Biennale in 2005.

Ina van Zyl (b. 1971) studied at
De Ateliers in Amsterdam and at Stellenbosch University, South Africa. Van Zyl's figurative work (painting, drawing and watercolours) is rendered with an intense sense of sensuality and oppression. Recent exhibitions include 'Highlighting Skin', De Ketelfactory, Schiedam, 2020; 'City in Sight', Amsterdam City Archives, 2019; 'Face Off Mondriaan vs. Contemporary Artists', Villa Mondriaan, Winterswijk, 2019; 'If There Were Water', Galerie Bernard Jordan, Paris, 2018, 'In a Landscape', Galerie Onrust, Amsterdam, 2014. Van Zyl lives and works in Amsterdam.

Design

Lotte Lara Schröder (b. 1988, Amsterdam) is an artist and graphic designer, interested in ecological and natural phenomena. Her 'free' work consists of drawings, paintings, and collages, often combined with sound or objects.

Lotte created the overall book and cover design, and the opening chapter images of this publication. These opening chapter pages are based on 'shame poles', a type of totem pole intended to publicly shame people. These poles are often placed in prominent locations and are removed once the wrong is corrected. Lotte freely used this idea of shame poles and layered these forms with collages inspired by images and themes from this book.

Publisher

Valiz is an independent international publisher, addressing contemporary developments in art, design, architecture, and urban affairs. Their books provide critical reflection and interdisciplinary inspiration in a broad and imaginative way, often establishing a connection between cultural disciplines and socio-economic questions. Valiz is headed by Astrid Vorstermans (1960) and Pia Pol (1985).

www.valiz.nl
@valiz_books_projects

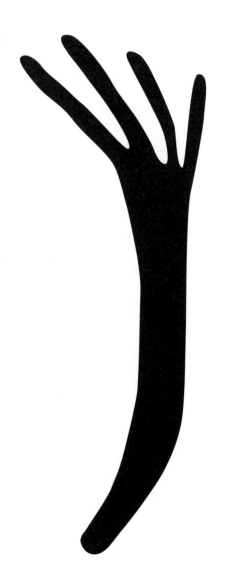

INDEX

SHAME! and Masculinity

COLOPHON

EDITOR
Ernst van Alphen

CONTRIBUTORS
Ernst van Alphen, Lorenzo Benadusi,
Jeannette Christensen, Marlene Dumas,
Adeola Enigbokan, Tijs Goldschmidt,
Arnoud Holleman, Hans Hovy,
Natasja Kensmil, Wahbie Long, Nalini
Malani, Maaike Meijer, Philip Miller,
Andrea Pető, Lotte Lara Schröder,
Artur Żmijewski, Ina van Zyl

COPY-EDITING
Leo Reijnen

TRANSLATION
Mieke Bal (Goldschmidt, Meijer)
Jennifer Newman (Benadusi)

PROOFREADING
Els Brinkman

INDEX
Elke Stevens, Nic de Jong

DESIGN
Lotte Lara Schröder
(incl. cover graphics, collages / 'shame
poles' at opening pages chapters)

PUBLISHER
Valiz, Amsterdam,
Astrid Vorstermans & Pia Pol,
www.valiz.nl

in partnership with H401,
Amsterdam, www.h401.org

H401 herengracht 401
research art dialogue

The project—H401's exhibition, the
public programme and Valiz' publication
—has kindly been supported by:
Mondriaan Fund
Prins Bernhard Cultuurfonds
Noord-Holland
LIRA
Creative Europe Programme of the
European Union

Co-funded by the
Creative Europe Programme
of the European Union

TYPEFACES

Kosmos by Mads Wildgaard/Bold-Decisions.biz
Jungka by Jung-Lee Typefoundry
Times New Roman MT Std

PAPER

Fedrigoni Arena Natural Rough 200 gr
Munken Print White 15 100 gr

PRINTING AND BINDING

Wilco Art Books, Amersfoort

This book has been produced on
FSC-certified paper.

DISTRIBUTION

NL/BE/LU: Centraal Boekhuis,
www.cb.nl
GB/IE: Anagram Books,
www.anagrambooks.com
Europe/Asia: Idea Books,
www.ideabooks.nl
USA/CA/Latin America: D.A.P.,
www.artbook.com
Australia: Perimeter,
www.perimeterdistribution.com
Individual orders: www.valiz.nl

PLURAL

The PLURAL series focuses on how
the intersections between
identity, power, representation and
emancipation play out in the arts
and in cultural practices. The volumes
in this series aim to do justice to
the plurality of voices, experiences and
perspectives in society and in the arts
and to address the history, present and
future meaning of these positions and
their interrelations. PLURAL brings
together new and critical insights from
artists, arts professionals, activists,
cultural and social researchers,
journalists and theorists.
Series design by Lotte Lara Schröder

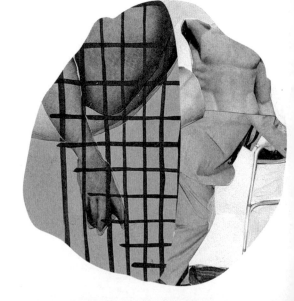

Shame! and Masculinity
is the second volume in the PLURAL series.

ISBN 978-94-92095-92-3
Printed and bound in the EU, 2020